The Teaching of History

Implementing the National Curriculum

Hilary Cooper

David Fulton Publishers

London

David Fulton Publishers Ltd
2 Barbon Close, London WCIN 3JX

First published in Great Britain by
David Fulton Publishers 1992

Note: The right of the author to be identified as the author of this work has been
asserted by her in accordance with the Copyright, Designs and Patents Act 1988.

Copyright © Hilary Cooper

British Library Cataloguing in Publication Data

Cooper, Hilary
   The teaching of history : implementing the national curriculum.
   I. Title
   907.1241

   ISBN 1-85346-186-5

Typeset by Chapterhouse, Formby, L37 3PX
Printed in Great Britain by BPCC Wheaton Ltd.

The Teaching of History
Implementing the National Curriculum

Contents

Foreword

Perhaps history is prone to sustain a burden of dullness because of its treatment of events in a distant past, events which appear to have little relevance to what we are told is the fast-changing world of today. When last week's news is regularly relegated to insignificance by the media, the affairs of the last century or millenium can so readily acquire a misty legendary quality. Since historical topics have also been handled in too many primary schools as a pot pourri of family memorabilia and visits to Roman villas, a fragmented presentation has left it with no coherent perspective.

Let us hope this state of affairs is itself due to become part of history, and it may well do so. Hilary Cooper certainly breathes life into the dead land, as her text conveys the exciting prospects for history in the National Curriculum. She sets down a persuasive rationale for the study of history in primary schools that includes a concern to develop as well as to inform the intellect. She shows how we can help children to weigh evidence to distinguish between very probable, probable and speculative explanations. She justifies rather than assumes the value of historical studies.

Taking into account the absurdities of an education system that expects primary teachers to be degree level specialists in one subject, generalists in the classroom, and instant experts in any new areas of need, Hilary Cooper provides extended illustrations of how named topics can be taught by non-specialists, if they are willing to be adventurous. So far as I know the approach is both original and radical; it is also sound. The text offers a brighter and better future for the study of the past.

Peter Robinson
January 1992

Introduction

Since September 1991, the National Curriculum has required history to be taught to all children throughout the five to eleven age-range. It was introduced against a background of extensive debate, in the media and amongst academic historians and teachers of history in schools. This debate was productive in focusing attention on the importance and nature of history in education. Often the debate was represented as a polarisation of 'facts' as opposed to the 'whys' and 'ifs' of learning history. Pamphlets from the Centre for Policy Studies (Beattie, 1987) appeared to echo Mr Gradgrind in *Hard Times*:

> Facts. Teach these boys and girls nothing but facts. Facts alone are what is needed in life. Plant nothing else and root out everything else... he seemed a galvanizing apparatus, charged with a grim mechanical substitute for the tender young imaginations that were to be stormed away.
>
> (Dickens, 1854)

The *History Workshop Journal* and Ruskin College, Oxford sponsored heated debates (1989, 1990) on a range of such issues. The History Curriculum Association was set up by academic historians to promote a traditional approach to school history. The Historical Association caused an outcry with its paper 'History in the Core Curriculum' (1987), which recommended sixty chronological topics for pupils from five to sixteen. However, after two rounds of eight lively and well-attended regional conferences in 1987 and 1988, a consensus was achieved amongst teachers in the Historical Association on the essential interaction of process and content, on criteria for defining these, and on the need for continuity and progression in developing and evaluating children's historical understanding. The structure of the National Curriculum for history reflects this achievement in that the content of the History Study Units must be

1

2

what the n.c has allowed to happen.

selected, taught and evaluated by teachers through the processes set out in the attainment targets. For the first time, it enables all children to learn history, in an increasingly complex way, through active problem-solving; it offers a framework for the development of Bruner's spiral curriculum in history (1963, 1966).

However, primary school teachers have not, on the whole, participated in this debate. There are many reasons for this. Few of them are history specialists. They have been over-burdened by the need to implement and assess the core subjects according to National Curriculum criteria, in rapid succession. This emphasis on the core subjects has conspired to reinforce the limited curriculum described in the ORACLE survey (Galton *et al.*, 1980). Moreover, although the Plowden Report (1967) advocated a broad and rich curriculum, much otherwise excellent practice during the last twenty years has echoed the emphasis placed by Bruner and Piaget on direct and concrete experiences; history has often been seen as remote and abstract, concerned with the affairs of adults and so not central to the experiences of young children, and too difficult for them to become actively involved in. The limited amount of research undertaken into young children's ability to understand the past has done little to dispel this idea, for reasons which will be discussed later. Consequently, although there have been some examples of excellent practice (Blyth, 1982, 1988; DES, 1989), history has not been widely taught in primary schools, and when it has been taught, it has often been based on television programmes and on copying from poor text books (DES, 1978, 1991; HMI Wales, 1989). There have been no clear aims, in terms of knowledge, skills and attitudes, and no consistent approach to planning and assessment.

It is important, however, to establish history as a key part of a broad primary school curriculum. Booth argued that

> We are part of our past experience, and we must seize all possibilities to perceive, grasp and possess this understanding by introducing children to history in such a way that it impinges on their consciousness and becomes part of their experience, so that they may be more truly themselves.

(Booth, 1969)

Nevertheless, there is a danger that, faced by the rapid succession of curriculum documents in the foundation subjects, teachers will find a holistic approach to primary education based on a broad integrated curriculum too complex to organise. Primary education may cease to be regarded as liberating and exciting, rooted in children's own experiences and enthusiasms and in problem-solving. Contrary to the intentions of the History Working Group, history may be perceived as a discrete discipline, driven by content and historiography, and on the periphery of social, emotional and intellectual development, rather than as central to it.

This book aims to show teachers, in a basic, practical way, how the National Curriculum for history may be implemented, developed, evaluated and ultimately modified in the light of existing good primary practice, by teachers who are, in the words of Blyth (1990), confident but not uncritical. It is based on the author's oblique involvement in the National Curriculum (as a member of the History Committee of the Schools Examination and Assessment Council, and of the Historical Association Schools Committee), on her work done with teachers and students, on research, and on her work with children over a long period, as a class teacher, throughout the four to eleven age-range.

The nature of historical thinking is discussed in Chapter 1 and Chapter 2 gives an overview of research relevant to young children's problem-solving in history. Chapter 3 considers the structure of the National Curriculum for history and how study units may be selected in a way which is compatible with a balanced, integrated curriculum. Case studies in Chapter 4 suggest how study units may be planned. Chapter 5 describes workshops in which teachers and students developed their own understanding of historical problem-solving. Chapter 6 outlines research undertaken by a class teacher, who investigates the effects of teaching strategies based on the discussion of sources, in the hope that other teachers may approach National Curriculum history in a similarly exploratory way.

CHAPTER 1

Historical Thinking

'Topic work' in primary schools has been criticised in the past as a rag-bag into which a confusion of content has been consigned, simply because it has tenuous links and involves a range of enjoyable activities. When history has been taught as a discrete subject, this has often been through didactic teaching from patronising secondary sources, which make generalised and stereotypical statements, and give no indication of the sources on which they are based, or of the area of uncertainty in interpreting the evidence which lies at the centre of any description or explanation of the past. The concepts of time and change, cause and effect, are rarely developed.

> After they had been there for four hundred years, the Romans went away. Their homes in Italy were being attacked by fierce tribes and every soldier was needed. The Britons were sad when they went, for they had no soldiers of their own to protect them from the sea-raiders who were growing bolder in their attacks upon the coast.
>
> (Unstead, 1964, p. 42)

Illustrations of artefacts are often presented as curious remnants rather than as rich sources from which a range of possible deductions may be made about the people who used them, and how their lives may have been influenced by them. 'Main events' and 'famous people' are listed at the back of a book simply because they happened, without apparent significance, and without conveying the idea that historians weave them together into accounts of the past, that they select and interpret them, and that this is why accounts may differ.

Children's active learning is assumed to occur through 'Things to Do' at the end of a chapter, but this rarely involves a reconstruction based on real historical evidence, a real building or an archaeological site, and the inevitable questions this would raise. It is more likely to suggest that you 'Make a model Viking ship from stiff card or paper, as

5

shown below...' (Mitchell and Middleton, 1967, p. 88). Alternatively, you may be asked to 'Pretend you are a merchant living in Saxon times and tell of your adventures', which presupposes an understanding of attitudes, values and a social structure quite different from our own, or else invites anachronism and identification and so inhibits the development of true historical understanding.

Secondary sources for children are often written in unnecessarily obscure language.

> Drake is the most famous mariner in English history. He is renowned for his adventurous exploits as well as his enterprising skill in establishing the English navy as the country's main national weapon.
> (Famous Sailors, 1970)

Yet it has long been recognised that from the very beginning, children should learn to grapple with the problems that lie at the heart of a discipline (Bruner, 1966; Pring, 1976; Lawton, 1975), and that they should do so in an increasingly complex way. What then are the thinking processes required by history? What are the questions historians ask, how do they answer them, and is this relevant to history in the primary school?

The content of history

As David Thomson (1969) explained, history has developed over the last two hundred years from chronicles of unrelated events into a discipline which aims to interpret different kinds of evidence in order to understand societies in the past. Its content is diverse: social, economic, constitutional, aesthetic. It may be concerned with individuals, institutions or groups. Philip Phenix (1964) saw history, with religion and philosophy, as forming a 'Realm of Meaning' which unites all other kinds of thinking. The National Curriculum takes account of this breadth of content.

It is the questions historians ask, however, and the ways in which they answer them, that distinguish history as a discipline. History is concerned with the causes and effects of change over time; with the ways in which, and the reasons why, societies in the past were different from ours, and what caused them to change. Historians investigate the past by interpreting traces of the past, the evidence. They interpret evidence through a process of deductive reasoning, but evidence is often incomplete, and for this and other reasons, more than one interpretation may be defensible. Producing a range of valid interpretations involves thinking which we may call 'historical imagination'. A wide and perceptive range of valid interpretations may eventually lead to an understanding of why people in the past may have thought, felt and behaved differently from us. Historical enquiry also depends on concepts which are, in varying degrees, peculiar to history. In this chapter, each of these aspects of historical thinking will be considered in turn. It is important to remember that they interact with each other in the process of finding out about the past.

The processes of historical problem-solving

Making inferences about the past from evidence

There are many kinds of historical evidence: oral history, artefacts, pictures and photographs, maps, statistics, writing. Written evidence is wide-ranging: documents, laws, tombstone inscriptions, diaries, newspaper accounts, contemporary literature. Making historical inferences involves forming arguments about the significance of a piece of evidence: what does it tell us about the society that produced it? How was it made? Why? What was it used for? By whom? Where was it found? Are there others? . . . and so on.

Superior examples of Roman shoes found at Vindolanda, the equivalent of shoes made by Gucci or Lobbe today, tell us something about the social and economic structure of the fort. A letter from a first generation 'Dutch' Roman at the fort, written in Latin, asking for underpants and socks from Rome, may tell us about the economic and transport systems of the empire, and the attitudes of Dutch tribes to the cold, clothes and culture.

Since there is a limit to what can be known for certain, a historian must also make inferences which are probabilistic – reasonable guesses about the evidence. The four post-holes in the centre of an Iron Age house plan may be to support the roof (Bersu, 1940), they may surround an open courtyard where animals could be kept (Clarke, 1960), or they may be a free-standing tower for repairing the roof (Harding, 1974).

If the evidence is incomplete, the historian must also be able to tolerate that which can never be known; for example, we do not know how much of a new style of agriculture the Romans introduced to Britain, or how it was related to the old, and so how British communities related to Roman villas, since no examples of Roman field patterns have been identified (Richmond, 1955).

This process of enquiry in interpreting historical evidence was clarified by Collingwood in his autobiography (1939). He proceeded from specific questions about the significance and purpose of objects (whether they were buttons, dwellings or settlements), to their meaning for the people who made them. For instance, he *knew* that a Roman wall from the Tyne to Solway existed. He *guessed* its purpose was to form a sentry wall with parapets as a protection against snipers. He *wanted to know* if there were towers as a defence against trying to land at Bowness or St. Bees, in order to support his guess. A search revealed that towers had been found, but their existence forgotten (because their purpose was not questioned).

Interpreting historical evidence involves not only internal argument, but also debate with others, testing inferences against evidence from other sources and considering other points of view. It means then supporting opinions with arguments, accepting that there is not always a 'right' answer, that there may be equally valid but different interpretations, and that some questions cannot be answered. This kind of thinking is as important to the social, emotional and intellectual growth of young children, as it is necessary in adult society.

Developing historical understanding

Interpreting historical evidence may involve suggesting how something was made, or used, or what it may have meant to people at the time. It may involve explaining a sequence of events or the behaviour of an individual or a group. Evidence is always incomplete. It is a reflection of the feelings and thoughts of the people who created it. Historical evidence is, therefore, often open to a variety of equally valid interpretations. In order to interpret evidence, it is necessary to understand that people in the past may have thought, felt and behaved differently from us, because they lived in societies with different knowledge-bases, belief-systems, views of the world, and different social, political and economic constraints.The disposition to make a variety of suggestions about incomplete evidence, which take into account that people in the past may have thought and felt differently from us, is therefore an integral part of making historical inferences. It has been called 'historical imagination' or 'historical empathy'. However, these terms have led to a great deal of confusion because they have often been regarded as the product of free-floating imagination discrete from interpreting evidence. They have also been confused with projecting oneself into the past, or with identifying or sympathising with people in the past. The historian cannot share the thoughts and feelings of people in the past but can attempt to understand and explain what these may have been. There has been confusion too, because the terms 'historical imagination' or 'empathy' involve a number of subordinate concepts: understanding different points of view in a conflict, the motives of an individual or a group, the values, attitudes and beliefs of another society.

Historians have an implicit understanding of historical imagination, which is usually not adequately articulated. Kitson Clarke (1967) pointed out that 'men's actions can be the subject of detailed research, but what went on in their minds can only be known by inference.' Elton (1970) saw historical imagination as 'a tool for filling in the gaps when facts are not available'. Ryle (1979) saw it as a means of cashing in on the facts and using them: ammunition shortage and heavy rain before a battle cause the historian to wonder about the hungry rifleman and delayed mule trains. Thomas (1983) said that what interests him about the past is what ordinary people thought, felt and believed. Collingwood (1939, p. 7) attempted to clarify the relationship between interpreting evidence and interpreting the thoughts and feelings of the people who made it. He says, for example, that we *know* that Julius Caesar invaded Britain in successive years; we can suppose that his *thoughts* may have been about trade, or grain supply, or a range of other possibilities, and that his underlying *feelings* may have included ambition or career advancement. (Mink (1968) rigorously analysed Collingwood's thinking on this subject in his article 'Collingwood's Dialectic of History'.)

Historians, then, do not question that making deductions about historical evidence involves probabilistic interpretations, and conjectures about thoughts, feelings and beliefs. Their job is not to reproduce the lost world of the past, but to ask questions and to try to answer them.

Nevertheless, it is important to recognise that suppositions about the feelings and thoughts of people who made and used historical evidence have to conform to criteria of validity. There must be no contradictory evidence. It must be assumed that people in the past acted rationally. Inferences must be supported by argument and conform to what else is known of the period. Historians must also attempt to understand what the evidence may have meant to people at the time. What, for example, was the status of a torc, dating from 1000BC, discovered in a Wiltshire field? 'This may have been a votive offering to a God, or buried as part of a funeral ceremony, or it might have been stored' (Merriman, 1990).

Children can take part in the process of making suggestions about how things were made and used and how the people who used them may have thought and felt. They can be helped to imagine, for example, how it may have felt to do the washing using a copper, a dolly, a scrubber and a flat iron, to go to bed by candlelight, or to wear the clothes of children depicted in an old portrait. They can use parish registers, census records, street directories, old maps and information about daily life from secondary sources to reconstruct the life of a particular family living in a particular house at a given time in the past. They can suggest what life may have been like in seventeenth-century London after reading extracts from Pepys' diary, or how a Roman villa they have visited may have looked when it was first built. But the imaginative conjecture must be rooted in the evidence.

Children must be encouraged to 'go beyond the evidence' because this is central to developing historical understanding. Therefore they must gradually learn through discussion with each other and with their teacher how to make interpretations which are historically valid.

Using historical concepts

Historical evidence can only be interpreted through language. In order to ask questions of evidence, we need to use concepts which are in varying degrees peculiar to history. As Blyth (1990) pointed out, however, lists of historical concepts are drawn up almost arbitrarily. Some concepts are concerned with space and time, some are methodological: similarity and difference, cause and effect, continuity and change. Other concepts are organising ideas which run through human society: communication, power, beliefs, conflict. Concepts are created by historians to encapsulate historical periods: Renaissance, Reformation, Victorian. There are 'closed' concepts which refer to a particular time (villa, elderman, Roundhead, Cavalier), and concepts which are not exclusively historical (trade, law, agriculture).

Children need to be given the opportunity explicitly to discuss historical concepts, and to use them in a variety of contexts in interactive situations because these concepts form the framework which makes historical enquiry possible.

Why is it necessary for children in the primary school to learn the processes of historical thinking?

It is impossible to learn history without learning the processes by which historians find out about the past. There is no one view of the past, and historians' accounts of the past differ. To understand history, it is necessary to understand why these differences occur. It is necessary to understand that evidence from which accounts are constructed is incomplete and so more than one interpretation is usually possible. Therefore, historians write accounts of the past which involve both selecting and interpreting evidence, in order to explain what happened and why. The areas they choose to investigate, the evidence they select, their interpretations of the feelings and thoughts which lie behind actions, and the patterns of events they construct often differ. They may vary as a result of the historian's interests, the concerns and philosophies of the times in which s/he lives, or the discovery of new evidence. A Marxist historian like Christopher Hill, for example, will write a different account of the English Civil War from that of C. V. Wedgewood. Recent historians (Fryer, 1984, 1989; Vishram, 1988; Rodney, 1972) have challenged an Anglocentric view of history. Others have taken a woman's perspective (Boulding, 1981; Beddoe, 1983; Rowbotham, 1973).

History is dynamic. In learning about the past through secondary sources, children will discover that accounts differ, and in asking their own questions about primary sources, they will begin to discover why. It is important to social and intellectual development, not solely to historical understanding, to realise that arguments must be supported and that there is often no one 'right' answer.

CHAPTER 2

Historical Thinking and Cognitive Development

Is it then possible for children to be involved in the processes of historical thinking in an increasingly complex way, and if so, how may this be achieved? In this chapter, we shall examine theories of cognitive development relevant to each aspect of historical thinking: making inferences, historical imagination, and concept development. Research which relates each area to children's thinking in history will also be discussed. Finally, we shall consider the implications of cognitive psychology and research into children's learning in history for the structuring of a history curriculum for young children.

Theories of cognitive development relevant to making historical inferences

Piaget posited a sequence in the development of children's thinking encompassing three qualitative stages. This is consistent with the view that children become increasingly able to make inferences about the past from historical sources. Young children, he found, were not able to hold more than one perspective at a time. At the next stage children's thinking was bound by observable reality. At the third stage they were able to hold in mind a range of hypothetical possibilities.

Piaget's work on time (1956) is not the most useful to apply to history. He investigated the development of concepts of time in relation to concepts of space, movement and velocity, through scientific experiments. Children were asked, for instance, to draw a succession of pictures showing water pouring from one container, through a spigot, into a container below. He found the first competency to emerge was the ability to match pictures of water in the upper and lower containers and put the pictures in order, showing an understanding of succession and order in time. Next children understood that the drop in one container and the rise in the other took the same amount of time to occur; they could understand temporal intervals between succeeding temporal points. At the third stage he found that children could understand that events can occur at the same time and also that temporal intervals can be added together. Then they become able to measure time as a temporal unit. Piaget suggested that it was not until this stage had been reached that children could understand 'lived time', 'age' and internal subjective time.

Piaget's research on probability and chance (1951) is also based on the manipulation of physical objects, predicting the colour of marbles to be drawn from a bag, or rolled down a tray. However, it is interesting that he found that while young children make no differentiation between chance and non-chance, at a concrete level children show an increasing awareness of what they can know and what they can guess, so that at a formal level, they are able to establish a firm bridge between the certain and the probable.

Piaget's work on language (1926) and on logic (1928) is the most helpful to apply to inferential reasoning in history. Here he sets out a sequence in the development of argument. In *The Language and Thought of the Child* (1926) he says that at the egocentric level, the child is not concerned with interesting or convincing others, and leaps from a premise to an unreasonable conclusion in one bound. Next s/he attempts to communicate intellectual processes which are factual and descriptive, and show incipient logic, but this is not clearly expressed. This leads to a valid statement of fact or description. From this follows 'primitive argument' in which the statement or opinion is followed by a deduction going beyond the information given, but the explanation for the deduction is only implicit. At the next stage, the child attempts to justify and demonstrate his assertion by using a conjunction (since, because, therefore), but does not succeed in expressing a truly logical relationship. Piaget says, in *Judgement and Reasoning in the Child*:

> The young child (7–8) rarely spontaneously uses 'because' or 'although' and if forced to finish sentences using them, uses them as a substitute for 'and then'.
>
> (Piaget, 1928)

The child eventually arrives at 'genuine argument', through frequent attempts to justify his own opinions and avoid contradiction, and as the result of internal debate, he is able to use 'because' and 'therefore' correctly to relate an argument to its premise. Finally, at a formal level, s/he can use not only conjunctions, but also disjunctions, can make implications and consider incompatible propositions.

This pattern in the development of argument has been examined, assessed and modified by subsequent research. Peel (1960) identified a 'describer' stage of unjustified and unqualified statements, a transitional stage of justified hypothesis and a recognition of logical possibilities, and an 'explainer' stage of weighed arguments using abstract propositions.

Nevertheless, young children's ability to make inferences may be greater than Piaget suggested. It often seems to be limited by lack of knowledge or experience, or failure to understand the kind of thinking that is expected. In history it would vary, depending on the nature of the evidence. Piaget and Inhelder themselves (Peel, 1960) found levels of thinking varied according to the nature of the questions asked.

A child's interest and involvement are also important as Beard (1960) showed. Isaacs (1948) found very young children capable of logical argument if they understood how to tackle the problem and were interested in it. Wheeler (Peel, 1960) found that logical thinking can exist from an early age, and that it becomes more complex through increased experience and memory. Piaget's own case studies offer some evidence that comments, suggestions and criticisms make pupils aware of the elements in problem-solving, and can accelerate their progress. Donaldson (1978) examined the dichotomy she recognised between children's capacity for reasoning in informal, everyday situations and Piaget's conclusion that children under seven have little reasoning ability. She found that young children are capable of deductive reasoning, that their problem-solving depends on the extent to which they can concentrate on language, and that language development is related to other non-verbal clues which are also brought to bear in problem-solving. She found that children may encounter difficulties because they do not always select relevant items in problem-solving, are easily distracted, and rarely discuss the meaning of words. She concluded that a child's understanding depends on whether the reasoning stems from the child's immediate concerns or is externally imposed, and also on the child's expectation of what the questioner wants to know. She said, therefore, that young children must be helped to develop their ability to reason and to make inferences as early as possible by recognising the abstraction of language, and by receiving the right kind of help in problem-solving. They must also become aware of the nature of different disciplines.

Psychologists' work on reasoning, then, suggests that young children may be helped to develop arguments about historical evidence if we teach them how. It suggests that we need to provide interesting, memorable learning experiences, ask simple, open-ended questions, and teach appropriate vocabulary.

Research relating psychologists' work on making inferences to children's thinking in history

There have been studies relating Piaget's developmental levels to children's historical thinking. However, they have found that the three levels can be revealed amongst a group of children of almost any age, because the nature of the evidence and the complexity of the questions influences children's level of response. Since the studies have usually involved older children, they are of limited value to primary school teachers. Nevertheless, they have been encouraging in recognising approaches to teaching history which have been successful, in establishing that young children enjoy making inferences about historical evidence, and in focusing attention on the quality of children's thinking rather than simply on fact acquisition.

In the 1960s, children's responses to historical evidence were classified in terms of Piagetian levels by Lodwick (1958 in Peel, 1960, p. 121), Thompson (1962), Peel (1960), Booth (1969), Hallam (1975) and Rees (1976). Lodwick's study is perhaps the most useful to those interested in young children because it involved visual evidence and did not depend on understanding individuals' motives, or on causation. He showed children between seven and fourteen a picture of Stonehenge and asked them three questions, for example: 'Do you think Stonehenge might have been a temple or a fort?' Their answers showed a gradual development from unreason to logic, then the use of supporting evidence, and probabilistic thinking. Eventually, they were able both to support a hypothesis that it was a temple, and also to argue as to why it was not a fort. The answers suggest that the development in reasoning is due, to some extent, to an increase in knowledge. More information might therefore have enabled the children to argue logically at an earlier age.

Thompson (1962) gave a mixed ability class of twelve-year-old boys background information about William the Conqueror, then gave them extracts from the *Domesday Book* and from the *Anglo-Saxon Chronicle*, and asked them why William had the survey carried out. This material is far more complex than that of Lodwick, because it involves written evidence, comparing two sources, and understanding both bias and motive. It also involves understanding a society with different rules. At a preoperational level replies showed misunderstanding of the information. At a concrete level children repeated information given in the chronicle. Formal responses showed awareness of uncertainty and probability, an understanding of the King's insecure position, and of his need not to be cheated of taxes. Piaget's work on rules and motives (1932) showed that by twelve years old, children can understand that rules can be changed, they take account of motive, and see that justice is relative. Piaget says this is achieved through comparing and discussing perspectives. However, Thompson (1962) seems to have found some children operating at a fairly low level because of the abstraction and complexity of the material, and also perhaps because he required a written response.

It is not surprising that Peel (1960) traced the same three Piagetian levels of response amongst a group of junior school children when he asked a far more simple question about a story. He told them the story of King Alfred and the cakes, and asked them, 'Could Alfred cook?' Indeed, this is hardly a historical question and requires no understanding of laws, motive, bias or of another society. Peel found that at seven, children's answers were often illogical ('Yes, he was King', or, 'No, he could fight'). At a concrete level, they would restate evidence in the story, but at a transitional level they may state what might be expected ('I shouldn't think so – at least not as well. He didn't pay attention to the cakes. If he had been a good cook he might have known when they'd be done.'). At a formal level, they may state a possibility not given in the text ('I don't know, because if anyone could cook and had something else on his mind, he might still forget the cakes'). Peel's responses might have been analysed in a more refined way, appropriate to the age-range if his categories had reflected Piaget's sequence in *The Language and Thought of the Child* (1959): egocentric, incipient logic, statements of fact, implicit deduction, incomplete causal relationship, genuine argument.

Booth (1969) constructed tests for thirteen- to fourteen-year-olds, designed to explore the nature of their knowledge of history. They were asked questions about time and change, and about the attitudes, ideas and beliefs represented by three religious buildings of different periods. They were also asked to compare and contrast people, events and photographs of houses from different periods. Booth, too, found that answers fell into three categories: those that had little or no comprehension of the material or the questions, those that referred to the information given but made little attempt to refer to historical material outside the question; and those that showed selection and critical thinking and related their work to other relevant knowledge. Such questions and material could easily be adapted for primary school children, and if related to a unit of study, would most likely receive responses at the two higher levels, although their answers may be different from those of thirteen-year-olds.

It seems that researchers tried to fit their children's responses into Piaget's three bands, irrespective of age-group or material, rather than ask simple, open-ended questions and see what patterns emerged.

It is interesting that Booth found more divergent thinking and flexibility when children were asked questions orally and pupils' questionnaires showed that they enjoyed class discussion, local history studies, and examining pictures, documents and maps, and disliked facts, generalisations and 'essay' writing.

In the 1970s, experiments and strategies were designed to see if children's thinking in history could be accelerated within the Piagetian model, by teaching methods. Hallam (1975) worked with nine- and thirteen-year-olds and Rees (1976) with twelve-year-olds.

Hallam taught 'experimental' classes through active problem-solving in role-play ('Imagine you are Henry VIII and say why you have decided to abolish the monasteries'), through asking questions about Cromwell's diary and discussing passages from historical texts. He found that the classes taught through active problem-solving performed at a higher level than the traditionally taught control group.

Rees (1976) also found that children's thinking skills in history could be developed if they were taught to explain rather than describe, and to be aware of uncertainty and motive, by switching perspective. His classes of twelve-year-olds compared favourably at the end of the term with a control group who were taught in a didactic way. Rees found three levels of response to his fairly complex material. Answers requiring inference were considered to be preoperational if no explanation was given, at a concrete level if only one explanatory reference was given, and at a formal level if all explanatory references were given. Responses to questions requiring pupils to take account of two points of view fell into three categories: those which showed no logic, those which showed increasing quantities of substantiating evidence but only in support of one viewpoint, and those that appreciated two viewpoints.

Dickinson and Lee (1978, p. 82) concentrated on defining historical thinking, rather than Piagetian levels, as the starting point. They made clear for the first time the important distinction between understanding behaviour from a contemporary viewpoint and from the standpoint available to the person at the time. They gave adolescents some of the information available to Jellico before the Battle of Jutland and asked them why he turned back. They traced a sequence in the development of the pupils' understanding that there is a difference between Jellico's point of view and that of the historian.

Shemilt (1980) worked with thirteen- to sixteen-year-olds. He found that children taught through active problem-solving are less inclined to regard 'facts' as certain. He suggested the following pattern of development: evidence as 'information', as giving answers to be unearthed, as presenting problems to work out, and finally as recognition that the context of evidence is necessary to establish historicity.

Although this research is interesting because it shows that it is possible to develop genuine historical thinking, it gives the impression that this is only possible with older children. However, with simpler material and questions, these approaches could be adapted for younger children. It seems important therefore to define, through teachers' experience, based on planning for precise learning outcomes, the historical questions and kinds of evidence appropriate at different ages, and to look, in a much more refined way at children's responses to them.

Shawyer, Booth and Brown (1988) noted that although there has been greater use of sources in the last ten years, there has been little research into children's levels of understanding of the evidence. Three recent small-scale studies have investigated young children's ability to make inferences about evidence; they did not attempt to explore the range of children's thinking in detail, but they do suggest that it is possible to teach strategies which stimulate the building blocks of advanced historical thinking in young children.

Wright (1984) found that classes of seven-year-old children could draw their own conclusions about pottery 'finds' from the past; Davis (1986) asked junior school children to identify 'mystery objects' and found they could make historical statements which were tentative and provisional. Hodgkinson (1986) showed genuine historical objects (e.g. newspapers, candle-holders) and 'fake' historical objects (e.g, mock ship's log), to children of nine and ten years old. He, too, found they used probability words and used 'because' to develop an argument. Marbeau (1988) concluded that in primary school history, we must provide a means for open and animated thought so that the child has intellectual autonomy, can take risks, exchange ideas and organise thoughts relative to the thoughts of others. In this way, a plan or a photograph can come to life.

Theories of cognitive development relevant to historical imagination and empathy

Confusion over what is meant by empathy in psychology is easily shown. Goldstein and Michels (1985) gave seventeen definitions, and Knight (1989b) refers to many more examples. However, there are three aspects of developmental psychology which seem relevant to the development of historical imagination and empathy: work on 'creative thinking', work on changing perspective, and theories of psychodynamics.

The first area, 'creative thinking', has implications for how children may best be encouraged to make a range of valid suppositions about evidence, (how it was made and used, and what it meant to people at the time).

Since the 1960s, psychologists who were concerned that traditional intelligence tests were too narrow a measure of intellectual ability, have devised creativity tests. Creativity however was also difficult to define. Rogers (1959) saw it as 'growing out of the interaction of the individual and his material'. Guilford (1959) listed traits related to creativity: the ability to see a problem, fertility of ideas, word-fluency, expressional fluency, and fluency of ideas (the ability to produce ideas to fulfil certain requirements such as uses for a brick, in limited time), flexible thinkers who could produce a variety of ideas, or solve unusual problems (which of the following objects could be adapted to make a needle – a radish, fish, shoe, carnation?), and tolerance of ambiguity, a willingness to accept some uncertainty in conclusions.

Guilford devised tests to measure such abilities. Other tests of creativity followed. Torrance (1965) used an 'Ask and Guess' test requiring hypotheses about causes and results related to a picture, and a 'just suppose' test in which an improbable situation in a drawing requires imaginative solutions. Wallach and Kagan (1965) said that creativity can be tested by the number of associates, and the number of unique associates generated in response to given tests, both verbal and visual. Their tests included interpretation of visual patterns and suggesting uses for objects such as a cork or a shoe. Researchers concluded that creativity is a dimension which involves a child's ability to generate unique and plentiful associates in a task-appropriate manner, and in a relatively playful context.

Such research has implications for classroom practice. It is generally accepted that the ability to think creatively rather than conform without question is important for individual and social well-being. Teachers can develop divergent thinking both through creative problem-solving courses (Parnes, 1959), and by creating an environment in which children become confident in their ability to think adventurously (Haddon and Lytton, 1968). On the other hand, Torrance (1962), Wallach and Kagan (1965), and Getzels and Jackson (1962) showed that highly creative children are often not encouraged or recognised by their teachers, who prefer conformity.

The second area of psychologists' work which may shed light on children's ability to understand how people in the past may have felt, thought and behaved is concerned directly with empathy. However, psychologists' definitions of empathy are of limited use when applied to history because they are partial, misleading or irrelevant. Piaget saw it as a cognitive process, thinking rather than feeling from someone else's point of view. His 'Three Mountains' experiment (1956) suggested that young children find this difficult, but others have said that it depends on their involvement, and on their understanding of the situation. J. H. Flavell (1985) suggested that children are capable of making inferences which enable them to see someone else's point of view, but do not see the need to do so. This is endorsed by Martin Hughes' 'Policeman Replication' of the Three Mountains experiment (Donaldson, 1978) and by the 'Sesame Street test' of H. Borke (1978).

Recent research differentiates between visual perspective-taking, conversational role-taking and pictorial representation, and in each instance, young children appear to be underestimated. Cox (1986) said that in their verbal interactions, young children do develop inferences concerning the points of view of others, but more research is needed into the intervening years between early childhood and maturity.

Piaget (1932) suggested the sequence in which children learn about rules: at first they do not understand that rules exist, then they change them according to their own needs. Next they come to accept one set of rules rigidly. Finally they are able to understand that rules change as society changes and are not absolute. In historical terms, they first become able to see life from another standpoint, but only with maturity can they understand that rules and behaviour change with society.

The third area of psychologists' work which has a bearing on how we should develop children's historical imagination is concerned with psychodynamics. Jones' (1968) approach was based on the work of

Erikson (1965). He criticised Bruner's emphasis on deductive reasoning, divorced from emotional involvement. Jones thought that children must be encouraged to understand both themselves and the behaviour, feelings and ideas of different societies and that it is essential that cognitive development should be related to emotional and imaginative growth. 'It is necessary that children feel myth as well as understand it' (1968, p. 49). He asked children, for example, to list the kinds of conflicts to be expected in a Netsilik winter camp and how they are solved (through food-sharing, games, taboos and magic), then to categorise their own conflicts and ways of solving them.

Theories relating to historical empathy regard it as both a cognitive and an affective process, although the relationship between these processes and the pattern of their development is unclear. Watts (1972) stressed the constant interaction of deductive reasoning with imaginative thinking in history. The work of some psychologists has shown that the creativity needed to make valid suppositions, and the ability to suggest another person's point of view requires reasoning, but psychodynamic theories show that such reasoning involves an exploration of creative fantasy, an understanding of our own feelings and of how these are part of shared human experience.

Research investigating the development of historical empathy in children

There have been three studies which suggest that in history, children become increasingly able to make suppositions, to understand other points of view and values different from their own.

Blakeway (1983) constructed tasks which she felt made 'human sense' (Donaldson, 1978), were age-appropriate (Borke, 1978), and which made children aware of different perspectives and of the need to communicate them (Knight, 1989c). In the first part of her study, she showed that her class of nine-year-olds could understand the pain and uncertainty of evacuees in the Second World War, and could also understand the thoughts and feelings which might have been experienced by an adult, a fighter pilot. However, the attempt to give the material 'human sense' in that it involved children not long ago, in the same school, meant that the children were more likely to sympathise and identify, than to display an understanding of different attitudes and values. In the second part of her study, she investigated the ability of two classes of eight- and nine-year-olds to make inferences. She asked them, 'What would you have felt if you were the fifteen-year-old King, Richard II, fighting the rebels in the Peasants' Revolt? Would you agree to their demands?' She found that the emotions ascribed to the King were limited to the children's own experience of life. This is not surprising since the difference between feeling fear, jealousy and anger depends on a person's perception of the situation. The older children offered *more* possible interpretations of the King's reasons and three-quarters of them were able to suggest why they might have gone to London, if they had been peasants. Blakeway's study (1983) shows that, by stopping to consider choice, children become aware of the possibilities that are available, they have control over their thinking, and become able to generate a variety of suppositions which lead towards understanding another point of view.

Knight (1989a,b) traced the emergence, in sequence, of four different aspects of children's understanding of people in the past. He tape-recorded 95 children between six and fourteen. He found that the first competency to emerge was the ability to retell a story from the point of view of someone involved in it. Six-year-olds found this difficult, but 67 per cent of the sample could do this by 9.3 years and 80 per cent by 10.3 years old. Next, children became able to explain an apparently strange attitude. They were told the story of General Wolfe, who died after finally capturing Quebec from the French. Then they were asked why he said 'Now I die happy'. Thirty-two per cent of six- and eight-year-olds offered nonsensical explanations, accepting that he was unaware of the dangers and also deterred by them. The older children (67 per cent by 9.4 years, 80 per cent by 12.8 years) accepted that people are driven by reasons and do what seems sensible to them and they also displayed an appreciation of a range of possibilities. The primary school children were not successful on the other two tasks, where they were asked to predict the ending of a story, and to interpret equivocal information about William I. Knight concluded, like Blakeway, that primary school children have sufficient understanding of people in the past to be worth encouraging, and that they are capable of making a range of valid suppositions. However, both these studies involve understanding accounts and motives of individuals in complex situations. It seems likely that attempts to understand the possible feelings and thoughts of people in the past begin to emerge much earlier.

Attempts to classify levels of historical empathy in adolescents have involved understanding of beliefs and complex social practices, and so have been less encouraging in their findings to primary practitioners. Ashby and Lee (1987) made video recordings of small-group discussions amongst eleven- to fourteen-year-olds, in which no teacher was present, about Anglo-Saxon oath-help and ordeals. At the first level, Anglo-Saxons were seen as simple, and their behaviour as absurd. At the next level, there are stereotyped role descriptions, with no attempt to distinguish between what people now know and think, and what they knew and thought in the past. At the level of every day empathy', there is a genuine attempt to reconstruct a situation and to project themselves into it and a recognition that beliefs, values and goals were different. At the fifth level, there is a clear understanding that people in the past had different points of view, institutions and social practices, and an attempt to understand what a person may have believed, in order to act in a particular way.

Research into young children's thinking in history suggests that, in a limited way, they can make suppositions about how people in the past may have felt and thought. However, this research has been concerned with motives and actions and has not investigated how children may make suppositions about evidence, artefacts, oral evidence, pictures or archaeological sites, in order to understand the thoughts and feelings of the people who made and used them.

Psychologists' research into the development of concepts

The wide-ranging nature of historical concepts and also the need for children to learn to use the vocabulary of history, has already been discussed (see p. 10). Psychologists have investigated both the sequence in which concept understanding develops and how concepts are learned, and this work has important implications for teachers.

Vygotsky (1962) showed that concepts are learned, not through ready-made definitions, but through trial and error, and experience. Concept development is a deductive process. The stages in which concepts are learned, not surprisingly, therefore correspond to those of Piaget. At the first stage, objects are linked by chance. At the second stage, they are linked by one characteristic, which can change as new information is introduced; children's and adults' words may seem to coincide but the child may be thinking of the concept in a different way; they may have a different understanding of what is meant by, for example, king, palace, peasant or law. At the final stage, a child is able to formulate a rule which establishes a relationship between other concepts and so creates an abstract idea; spears, daggers, guns, missiles are used for *defence* and *attack*; they are *weapons*. Klausmeier and Allen (1978), Klausmeier *et al.* (1979), Ausubel (1963, 1968) and

Gagné (1977) endorsed this process and the levels of understanding, with 'concrete' and directly experienced concepts preceding abstract ones, although this is not always the case, or true for all concepts.

Vygotsky suggested that concept development can be promoted by careful use of language. It is particularly significant for teachers of history that he said that concepts which are specially taught because they belong to a particular discipline and are not acquired spontaneously are learned more consciously and completely. The significant use of a new concept promotes intellectual growth. Shif (1935) found that in social studies, when given sentence fragments ending in 'because', more children were able to complete the sentence using a concept consciously learned than using a spontaneous concept related to family situations. They understood 'exploitation' better than 'cousin'. He concluded that this was because the teacher had encouraged them to use 'because' consciously and explained new concepts, supplied information, questioned and corrected, and so these concepts had been learned in the process of instruction in collaboration with an adult.

Klausmeier et al. (1979) discussed how concrete, tangible concepts are learned through verbal labelling and through storing images; for example through discussing the characteristics of Tudor houses, the different parts of the timber frame, the wattle, brick, thatch, jetties, pargeting, and by storing images of a range of different examples, language both connects and differentiates the images. As children get older, language becomes more important than visual and tactile perceptions. Abstract concepts are formed by asking a series of questions: What is an axe, a scraper, a flake or an awl used for? Why? How? What is their common purpose? What is a bow, harpoon, spear used for? Why? How? What do they have in common? Then the former are 'tools' and the latter are 'weapons'. Concepts such as 'control' or 'power' involve understanding subordinate abstract concepts; understanding things which give people power (concepts such as tools and weapons), things that have power over people (fear of hunger, illness, natural phenomena), and also the things people might quarrel about.

Research has shown then that concepts are best learned if they are selected and specially taught through illustrations, using visual or tactile examples of concrete concepts, and discussion of abstract concepts. Psychologists have therefore also considered the kinds of material children should be given to discuss and how these discussions may be promoted.

Bruner (1966) postulated three modes of representation in understanding a body of knowledge: 'enactive', depending on physical experience or sensation (a visit to a site maybe or using a tool or other artefact), 'iconic', when the essence of the experience is represented in pictures in the mind's eye (paintings, maps, diagrams, models), and 'symbolic', when concepts are organised in symbols or in language. He saw these three kinds of understanding as complementary rather than rigidly successive. Bruner (1963) said that the questions children are asked about the material must be not too trivial, not too hard, and must lead somewhere, and that we need to know more about the ways in which this can be done. He said that this needs particularly sensitive judgement in history, which is characterised by uncertainty, ambiguity and probability. They must be asked about carefully selected evidence, so that general principles can be inferred from specific instances, connections can be made, and detail can be placed in a structured pattern which is not forgotten. A young child, he said, must be given minimal information, and emphasis on how s/he can go beyond it. Having selected the experience, material and questions carefully, the child must also be shown how to answer them. Learning a particular way of formulating and answering questions may be an essential step towards understanding conceptual ideas.

Little has been done to put these principles into practice. Recent reports (DES, 1978, 1982, 1989) show that children are seldom taught to present a coherent argument, explore alternative possibilities, and draw conclusions. However, since the invention of the small, portable tape-recorder, there has been considerable research investigating discussion. There is evidence that a tape-recorder encourages 'on-task' behaviour and clear expression of ideas (Barnes and Todd, 1977; Richmond, 1982; Schools Council, 1979).

Piaget argued (1932, 1950) that conflicting viewpoints encourage the ability to consider more than one perspective at a time, and Vygotsky (1962) saw the growth of understanding as a collective process. Rosen and Rosen (1973, p. 32) and Wade (1981) discuss the nature of group conversations with or without the teacher. Indeed, there is evidence that if children are taught the kinds of questions to ask and appropriate ways of answering them, their discussions without the teacher are in many ways more valuable. Biott (1984) found that such discussions were more dense, discursive and reflective. Prisk (1987) found that when the teacher was present in an informal group, children did not use their organisational skills since the teacher was responsible for 80 per cent of the structuring moves. She found that open, unled discussion encouraged children to produce tentative suggestions and to explore ideas, entertain alternative hypotheses, and evaluate each other's contribution. Nevertheless, adult–child interaction is important if it is not used to transmit didactic information, but in order to help children to understand a question and how to answer it.

Current research argues that cognition is intrinsically social. Hamlyn (1982) argued that discussion is necessary, though not sufficient for knowledge: 'To understand that something is true presupposes knowing what is meant by true.' This involves appreciation of standards of correction and so implies correction by others, and so the context of personal relations. Knowledge is also always a matter of degree in the sense that two people may know 'x' (in 1492 Columbus sailed the ocean blue), but one may know more of why this is significant than the other. They may both know that Charles I was beheaded in 1649 but one may understand more of the reasons why. Doise *et al.* (1975), Doise (1978) and Doise and Mugny (1979) saw cognitive growth as the result of conflict of viewpoint and of interaction at different cognitive levels. Ashby and Lee (1987) found that children reached higher levels of understanding when arguing out a problem amongst themselves than they could achieve on their own, both in class discussion and in small group work, providing they had some strategy for tackling it. So far, there are no sensitive measures for assessing the effect of social interaction on cognition, but Light (1983, p. 85) concludes that we shall see rapid development in our understanding of these issues in the next few years.

There is much evidence however that structured discussion, using learned concepts is essential to the development of historical understanding (despite the findings of the ORACLE survey (1981) and the DES (1983) that very few opportunities were provided in schools for collaborative group work and extended discussion).

Discussion is more important in history than in other subjects because 'evidence', although it may be an artefact or a picture, can only be interpreted through language; it cannot, as in mathematics or science, be physically manipulated to investigate problems. Stones (1979) stressed the importance of teaching concepts, the stages involved, and the strategies for doing so: presenting examples and verbal feedback and encouraging the use of the concept in different situations.

Oliver (1985) concluded that if we are to appreciate the significance of evidence, there must be argument in order to reach conclusions and this must involve abstract concepts, although they will inevitably be rudimentary and incomplete.

Research applying theories of concept development to children's use of historical concepts

There have been studies investigating children's understanding of historical concepts: concepts of time, concepts often used in history but not related to a particular period, specifically historical vocabulary, and concepts related to the processes of historical thinking.

First let us consider research dealing with children's concepts of time. The work of Piaget (1956) suggested that since the concept of time can only be understood in relation to concepts of speed, movement and space and since understanding this relationship develops slowly, young children cannot understand that time can be measured in equal intervals. They cannot understand how long situations may last in relation to each other, or the sequence or coincidence of events. It was therefore often implied that history is not a suitable subject for young children. Peel (1967) concluded that young children cannot understand the nature of history or the significance of time within it. They may understand that William I became King, but not the implications of his reign or the place in historical time into which it fits.

Other researchers have considered the cultural, intellectual and philosophical implications of the concept of time, and asked how central this concept is to historical understanding. Jahoda (1963) said that conceptions of time and history depend on the social and intellectual climate; they are subjective. This approach had been illustrated in a study by Bernot and Blancard (1953). They showed how farm labourers in a French village, whose families had lived there for generations, had a perspective which went beyond their personal experience, whereas immigrant glass-blowers from itinerant families who moved into the village were almost without a sense of the past. People's different perspectives are clearly important in a local study. Children on a new suburban estate, or in an area with a large number of immigrants, will have different perspectives of the past from those in an isolated, long-established rural community.

The concept of time is cultural as well as subjective. The doings of Cromwell, the Act of Union, and the Famine of 1847 may seem more recent to an Irishman than to an Englishman.

Lello wondered whether, since time is not a natural and self-evident order, it really matters that a historical incident should be fixed in context and time. 'Is Herodotus devalued because his chronology is imaginary? Is Thucydides inferior because dates and chronology are almost ignored?' (1980, p. 344). Leach (1973) pointed out that the preoccupation of the early Christian authors with a numerical point of view was not in order to record dates, but because of their obsession with number logic. (This is seen, for example, in the representation of time, space and symbolism in The Westminster Pavement in Westminster Abbey.) If this view had not been abandoned, most modern development, especially science, could not have occurred. However, the implication of the change is that time is now inextricably linked with number in Western culture.

Lello concluded that chronology, though of undoubted importance, is not intrinsic to an understanding of time or history.

> Knowledge and a grasp of chronology are by no means synonymous with historical sense. Teaching history involves coming to terms with particular ways of explaining time to children which could, and sometimes does, run the risk of moulding children into preferred patterns of thinking, just as a rigid school time-table segments the day into artificial boxes.
>
> (1980, p. 347)

Smith and Tomlinson (1977) studied the understanding of historical duration of children between eight and fifteen. Children were asked to construct two historical intervals from their own knowledge of historical persons and/or events, to make absolute and comparative judgement of their durations, and to provide a rationale for these judgements. First the child was asked to name a historical person or event, then to work backwards or forwards from this anchor point, in one direction at a time, providing a minimum of three items coming 'just before' or 'just after' that in order to define a subjective historical period. The researcher wrote the items on cards. The child was then asked, 'how long do you think that took in history – a very long time, a long time, not very long, a short time, a very short time?'. The same process was repeated with respect to a second historical period, and the child was asked to compare the durations of the two intervals. S/he was asked to arrange the first set of cards in order. The second set was arranged beneath them by the researcher to cover the same distance, and the child was asked, 'Which of the two sets of historical items do you think took longest? How could you tell?'. Analysis revealed a sequence of responses:

(1)   arbitrary;
(2)   those equating historical intervals with the number of items (well, er, there's more things happened);
(3)   those which related the duration to the number of items of a particular type (the longest was the one with the most kings and queens), or to the amount of activity (modern wars are over quicker. Look at the weapons);
(4)   a recognition of a need for an independent scale, such as calendar years;
(5)   the child is able to overlap synchronous and partially overlapping intervals, and consistently apply an equal interval scale.

The value of such a study is that, having recognised a sequence of development, teachers are able to focus more clearly on the stage of a child's understanding and so to accelerate it. West (1981) found that children have a great deal of information about the past which they have not learned in school, and this enables them to sequence artefacts and pictures quite competently. Crowther (1982) investigated children's understanding of the dynamics of stability and change. He found that seven-year-olds regard change in terms of direct actions performed and as the substitution of one thing for another, taking little account of the time factor involved, but gradually children see change as part of the universal order of things, of transformation and gradual development, recognising succession and continuity in change, although they show less understanding of the disintegrating effects of change. As one eleven-year-old said, 'Everything alters in different times and different ways. Change can be dramatic; it can come gradually and you hardly notice it at all.'

Other researchers have investigated concepts loosely related to history. Not surprisingly, they traced three broad levels of development. Coltham (1960) chose 'king', 'early man', 'invasion', 'ruler', 'trade' and 'subject'. She asked children between nine and thirteen years old to draw what each concept conveyed to them, to choose the picture they thought conveyed the concept best from six pictures of each concept representing different levels of understanding, to define it verbally, and to choose appropriate doll's clothes to represent the concept. She found that at first, children depended on visual information and personal experience; later they were able to co-ordinate different points of view with their own experience, and at the highest level they showed awareness that concepts change with time.

Da Silva (1969) gave children a passage in which 'slum' was recorded as a nonsense word and asked them what they thought this nonsense word meant. At the lowest level, he found no attempt to use clues in the text, then a logically constructed response although the meaning changed with the context, and finally a level of deductive conceptualisation, when each piece of evidence was weighed against the others, and a stable definition for the nonsense word was achieved.

Booth (1979) asked secondary school children to group pictures and quotations related to 'Imperialism' and 'Nationalism' and classified their responses as concrete if the groups were based on physical facts in the evidence, such as colour of skin and abstract if they inferred relationships. He found responses were influenced by good teaching, interest and parental involvement. Furth (1980) also postulated landmarks in the development of children's understanding of the social world. He asked children between five and eleven, questions about social roles, money, government and communities. Their answer indicated a growing understanding of these concepts, from seeing society as unrelated individuals, to a grasp of a concrete, systematic framework, at eleven. He showed, for example, that at five, the primary cause for taking on a role is seen as a personal wish, but between five and seven, children stress the notion of order, and by eleven they focus on the idea of succession ('I suppose if someone leaves, someone comes') and the expertise inherent in a role ('Nearly every job you do, there has to be a man in charge'). Similarly, with government, children first had an image of a special man, then of a ruler, then of a job-giver or owner of land, until at nine or ten they understood that a government provides function and services in return for taxes.

Research, then, has shown how concepts develop through a process of generalisation, by storing an image of abstracted characteristics, and of deduction, by drawing from the stored image, adding to it and modifying it. It has indicated a pattern in the development of concepts, suggested that concepts need to be taught, and that they are best learned through discussion.

Implications of research for structuring the history curriculum

In the past, primary school history was widely presented as hard facts, not related to source material, described, not explained or analysed. Understanding of different values and beliefs was ignored. There was no clear framework for continuity and progression, which defined the nature of history and its contribution to the school curriculum. There was no method of assessment which was not dependent merely on increased information.

Research, though piecemeal and insufficient, has suggested that young children are capable of genuine historical problem-solving, that they are able to think historically in an increasingly complex way, and that language is an essential element in this process.

There have been a variety of suggestions about how young children may be involved in active learning in history. Palmer and Batho (1981) suggested that children may be taught to select relevant facts from a document, and Cowie (1985) advocated the use of sources 'to provide the slow learner with an opportunity for logical thought'. The Schools Council Project (1975–1980) suggested that children should learn to distinguish between fact and opinion and to see how and why evidence is biased and limited. It said, too, that they should learn to discuss similarities and differences, values and beliefs, in order to infer the feelings and actions of people in the past. The DES (1986) said that children should be shown objects and pictures, and encouraged to ask: What is it? What was it for? Who made it? Why? What difference did it make? What does it tell us about life in the past? Children should then gradually learn not to generalise from false premises, based on inadequate evidence, and that judgements are always provisional and tentative.

Blyth (1982) thought that young children could appreciate how the past was different by looking at, for example, a picture of a seventeenth-century dinner table and comparing it with their own. The Schools Council (1975–1980) suggested that older children may be shown a railway bill and make decisions on the basis of evidence that would have been available at the time.

Egan (Blyth, 1982) said that between four and nine years of age, children are aware of stark opposites of courage and cowardice, security and fear, life and death, and should be fed on classical stories, myth, and legend. The Schools Council (1975–1980) similarly said that between five and eight years, children should learn to differentiate between heroes and villains through stories which illustrate dilemmas and constraints formed through limitations of knowledge, wealth and geographical environment.

Phenix (1964) believed that children learn how values and beliefs change through learning about humanitarian reforms, about moral philosophers, and about laws and customs which describe ideal conditions, such as 'The Bill of Rights'.

However, these ideas for active learning in history are not related to patterns of development traced by cognitive psychologists. Bruner (1963) set out principles for structuring a discipline so that the thinking processes and concepts which lie at the heart of it can be tackled from the beginning, then in an increasingly complex form. He said this required translating the subject into appropriate forms of representation, which place emphasis on doing, and on appropriate imagery or graphics, and that a sequence of complexity in tackling these key questions and concepts must be defined. He said (1966) that this involved leading the learners through a series of statements and restatements that increase their ability to grasp and transfer what they have learned. Problems, he said, must involve the right degree of uncertainty in order to be interesting, and learning should be organised in units, each building on the foundation of the previous one. Finally, we must define the skills children need in order to learn effectively and so move on to extrapolate from particular memorable instances and to transfer the skills learned to other similar problems. This gives confidence and prevents 'mental overload'. Bruner (1963, Ch. 4) believed that 'the more elementary a course and the younger its students, the more serious must be its pedagogical aim of forming the intellectual powers of those whom it serves.' 'We teach a subject not to produce little living libraries, but to consider matters as an historian does, to take part in the process of knowledge . . . ' (Bruner, 1966, p. 22).

Bruner was aware, however, that much work was needed to provide detailed knowledge about the structuring of the humanities, and that this has been postponed in the past on the mistaken grounds that it is too difficult. The National Curriculum may be seen as an attempt to structure the thinking processes and concepts which lie at the heart of history in an increasingly complex way.

CHAPTER 3

The Implementation of the National Curriculum for History: A Whole-school Approach

In the National Curriculum for History the different aspects of historical thinking are described in the three attainment targets. Attainment target 1 is concerned with understanding change. It has three strands: understanding different kinds of change, understanding the causes and consequences of historical events and developments, and understanding the distinctive characteristics of societies in the past. Attainment target 2 involves understanding how accounts of the past are constructed and why different interpretations are possible. Attainment target 3 is concerned with making valid inferences from sources. Progression in each attainment target is posited in Statements of Attainment across ten levels. Levels 1–3 apply to key stage 1 and levels 2–5 to key stage 2.

These processes of historical thinking must be applied to the content specified in the programmes of study. In key stage 1, there is only one programme of study. It is concerned with myths and legends, stories about and eye-witness accounts of historical events, with fictional stories set in the past, and with changes in everyday life which children should find out about through a range of historical sources.

Key stage 2 consists of compulsory core study units based on particular periods, and is extended and complemented by selected supplementary units which must involve a theme over at least a thousand years, a unit based on local history, and a past non-European civilisation. The programmes of study for Wales are slightly different from those for England, requiring that pupils should be taught about 'important developments in the history of Wales and Britain': there is a compulsory study unit (study unit 2) on 'Early Peoples: Prehistoric, Celtic and Roman Britain', whereas in England, prehistoric and Celtic peoples are not specified, and in Wales, the units on Victorian times and on this century specify 'Life in Wales and Britain'. (Indeed, 1900–1930 is omitted in the English study units.)

Pupils should have the opportunity to use a range of historical sources: written evidence, artefacts, pictures and photographs, music, buildings and sites, and computer-based materials (National Curriculum for History, 1991, p.16). They should also be introduced to a range of perspectives: political, economic, technological and scientific, social, religious, cultural and aesthetic (1991, p.15). In each of the core programmes of study (and also in the supplementary units in the Welsh document), the key issues, events and personalities which children should learn about are set out with commendable economy. A section on historical enquiry and communication (1991, p.17) shows how pupils may be actively involved in the processes of historical investigation which stem from their own interests, through asking questions, selecting and recording their own sources, organising the information they collect and investigating and presenting it using a range of techniques: oral, model-making, collages, drama, and information technology. Pupils must study nine of the study units over the four years of the key stage, but there is no requirement that they should be taught in a particular order (although this is recommended (Non-Statutory Guidance C4.2)). Links between history and other subjects, and cross-curricular themes should be explored.

The National Curriculum thus recognises the essential relationship between process and content, and the importance of pupils being helped to ask questions which interest them and find out how to investigate them. It allows for depth studies and broad brush-strokes, for links between local, national and world dimensions. There are opportunities for creativity on the part of teachers. Firstly, in this chapter, we shall consider how to decide whether history is to be taught through an integrated curriculum or as a discrete subject. Secondly, key stage 1 will be discussed, the possible focuses within it, and activities based on those which are related to the attainment targets at the first three levels. This will be compared with the planning of activities for a local study for key stage 2 (supplementary unit B), across levels 3 to 5. Finally, six stages will be suggested for planning and implementing key stage 2 and decisions to be made will be examined.

History within an integrated curriculum or as a discrete subject?

The National Curriculum for history was, in some ways, intended to prevent history being included in broad topics such as

'Communications', 'Forces', 'Patterns' or 'Change', which did not give due attention to the processes of historical thinking, or to criteria for selecting historical content. Such topics have proliferated in recent attempts to teach the National Curriculum for science in an integrated way. There is a danger that many schools, having incorporated science into an integrated curriculum will accommodate history (and geography) by 'bolting them on' as discrete subjects, and the integrated primary curriculum advocated by Plowden (1967) will be abandoned.

However, there is no reason why a core history study unit should not itself form the basis of an integrated curriculum for one term during each year. Firstly, it could be argued that this is by far the best way to teach it. History is an umbrella discipline. Changes in attitudes to mathematics and in science and technology lie at the heart of social change which is in turn reflected in cultural and aesthetic changes. Secondly, language and mathematics are themselves communications systems for describing, investigating, representing and expressing problems and issues both now and in the past. The National Curriculum for mathematics, science and technology stresses the importance of 'using and applying' these disciplines. If at some points during the school year, a history focused topic can become the core of the curriculum, this will allow the opportunity to get really immersed in a period in far greater depth, because there is more time, and there are richer methods of investigation. Education is primarily concerned with learning about people and society in all its aspects, and it could be argued that the humanities should lie at the core of education. In debating the National Curriculum for history in Parliament (*Hansard* 29.4 1991, p. 136) Patrick Cormack regretted that history is not a core subject, and hoped that it will become so.

In this section, we shall consider briefly the areas in which other disciplines can be related to historical content.

I   *Mathematics*
(i)   *Shape and space*
      Properties of two-dimensional shapes:
      identify shapes in buildings: windows, doors, pediments.
      Properties of three-dimensional shapes:
      identify cuboids, cubes (buildings, steps), prisms (roofs), cylinders (pillars, chimneys); measure, reduce to scale, make nets and models of buildings.
      Maps, journeys, plans of sites.

(ii) *Number/algebra/symmetry*
Repeating patterns: windows, railings, terraces.
Tesellations: brickwork, tiles, mosaics, garden design, wallpaper, fabric.

(iii) *Measures. Length/distance*
Measure routes (scale).
Time, speed and distance calculations.
Measure buildings.
Record size (e.g. of ships) by drawing on ground.

Time
Time zones, devices for calculating solar time.
Different ways of measuring time (sand clocks, water clocks, candle clocks).
Different ways of recording time (Chinese, Indian, Arabic, European calendars), agricultural calendars, ships' logs, school and factory time-tables, diaries.
Changing attitudes to and effects of precise measurement of time.

Weight
Recipes, rations, diet.
Weight of load carried (e.g. coal carried by child labourer).
Weight of cattle and sheep at beginning and end of eighteenth century.
Capacity (e.g. how much beer drunk daily at Hampton Court in reign of Henry VIII).

Money
Price of food, proportion of income.

(iv) *Number calculations and estimations, data collection, presentation and interpretation*
Statistics
Census returns
Street directories
Graveyard studies
Parish records
Population statistics
Trade figures
Questionnaires and surveys

Time-lines
Counting systems in other cultures
Information about journeys can often be found in diaries, letters and oral accounts, advertisements for stage coaches, newspapers and old time-tables. Statistics about trade or population figures

can be extracted from books written for adults. Calculations can be used to investigate historical questions.

II *Language*
(i) *Speaking and listening*
Discussion of evidence, using selected concepts: (how was it made, how does it work, what does it tell us about the past, is it a reliable source? Supporting points of view with argument).
Interviews and questionnaires.
Listening to fiction about the past, listening to stories, myths, legends, accounts.
Presenting findings as slide shows or on video or oral tape, or directly to audiences of children, parents or other members of the community.
Discussion of how to interpret evidence (e.g. while model-making, drawing).
'Home corner' play using old artefacts.
Drama, role-play, debate (did the Ancient Greeks treat women fairly?), improvising stories, puppet plays, 'hot-seating', (what would you do next?), freeze-frames based on a picture (who are you? what are you doing?).
Listening to video or oral tape-recordings.

(ii) *Reading*
Reading visual images (films, books, photographs).
Making books, brochures, posters to present findings (individual, group or class).
Reading stories about the past (consider viewpoints, motives, how true the story may be).

(iii) *Writing*
Note-taking from teacher's presentation: from reference books.
Labels to explain what models, drawings, historical sources, tell us about the past (e.g. in a class museum).
Quizzes about evidence (e.g. a museum trail).
Letters (e.g. to museums and galleries or to invite visitors to the school).
Directions (e.g. for other visitors to a site or gallery).
Stories, plays, poems, based on evidence, describing and explaining the past.
Writing presenting a point of view (how true is this diary account?).
Reviews of stories about the past.
Shared writing (e.g. working in groups to write newspapers from different viewpoints).
Writing about science investigations connected with history topic.

40

III Science

(i) *Materials*

Used to make toys, buildings, transport, clothes, tools and machines; what are their properties, where do they come from, how have they changed, why?

(ii) *Processes of life*

Health, hygiene, diet, medicines, now and in the past.

How have they changed? Why? What have been the effects of changes?

(iii) *Genetics and evolution*

Selective growth of crops and breeding of domestic animals; changes in food and farming.

(iv) *Earth and atmosphere*

Influences of climate, rainfall, wind direction, soil-type on settlement.

(v) *Forces*

Tools, machines, transport, buildings.

(vi) *Electricity and information technology*

Effects on daily life (e.g. of domestic appliances).

(vii) *Energy*

Toys; how do they work?

Wind, water, steam, nuclear power; effects on way of life, causes and effects of change.

(viii) *Sound and music*

Musical instruments in the past; how did they work?

Music, what did it sound like, who played/listened; when?

Song, dance.

(ix) *Light*

Scientific revolution: lenses, telescopes, new ideas about the earth in space.

IV Art

Study of contemporary paintings and design.

Observational drawing, developed in other media: painting, printing, embroidery.

Design based on detail in fabric, ceramics, furniture, or in building materials (wood, brick, stone, iron). (Printing, computing.)

Model-making in junk, balsa wood (e.g. timber-frame building), pottery, in order to reconstruct an artefact, building, street or site from available evidence.

V Technology

Model-making; making 'props' for role-play or for class museum, or for acting out a story; grinding seeds, making dough, cooking recipes from period; carding, spinning, weaving, dying wool; drawing plans of artefacts, or buildings, using simple machines or tools from the past (e.g. candle snuffer, button hook); copying old designs in fabric, needlework, wallpaper, mosaics, pottery.

VI *Geography*
(i) Making and reading maps.
(ii) Understanding places, reasons for settlement; climate, relief, resources.
(iii) Communication between settlements; social, economic, aesthetic.
(iv) Reasons for changes in settlements or populations.

VII *Religious education*
Belief systems, celebration of beliefs (places of worship and festivals), effects of beliefs on individuals and communities.

It is clearly not possible to make history consistently the focus of a crowded curriculum; yet the prescribed content of the history curriculum makes it essential that some topics are taught with a clear history focus. The solution within an integrated approach, seems to be to teach a core study unit during one term of each year through an integrated topic with a strong history focus. During the other two terms, units can be chosen which introduce or develop the core unit as part of either a science-focused or a geography-focused topic. Work with a science and technology focus on forces, energy or materials, would link well with the history thematic units (category A supplementary units), or work with a science focus on human influences on the earth, or the variety and processes of life could link with a local history study unit (category B supplementary units). Topics with a geography focus on the local area could also link with a local history study. A geography study of a contrasting area in the UK could link with any of the British history units. A locality in an economically developing country could be linked with core study units 2, 3 and 4, or with some category C supplementary units. A locality in the European Community outside the UK could be linked with any of the core study units.

Key stage 1 and key stage 2, supplementary unit B

Although key stage 1 is concerned with local and family history and with stories and legends, there are a range of different focuses and

Table 3.1: Key stage 1

	Starting point (evidence)	Activity	Assessment AT1	AT2	AT3
Family	Photographs	Collect photographs of self/family. Put them in sequence/on a time-line. Describe changes, similarities and differences.	2c 3ac		1,2,3
	Artefacts	Collect 'old things'. Make a museum. Try to place exhibits in sequence. Explain what they tell us about the past.	2ac 3abc		1,2,3
	Visit site, museum, gallery: Site what happened here . . . ? Museum what is it for? How is it made/used?	Site: role-play, models, plans, drawings, stories.	1ab 2bc	1,2,3	1,2,3
		Museum: drawings, explanations, use/examine artefacts.	3abc 1a 2abc 3abc	3	1,2,3
	Gallery clothes, furniture or narrative, in paintings.	Gallery: role-play, stories about pictures (wear clothes – e.g. Geffrye Museum). Sort and name materials in clothes.	1ab 2bc 3abc	1,2,3	1,2,3
	Oral	Questionnaires, interviews, film and video	1ab 2bc 3abc	2,3	1,2,3
Locality	Buildings (houses, shops, church, farm, offices, civic buildings) Photographs, paintings, old postcards	Observe changes in structure, materials, purpose: draw, model, photograph. Look for what they tell us about the past, similarities and differences.	1a 2abc 3abc	2,3	1,2,3
	Maps Oral	Look for differences, explain. Interviews, questionnaires, stories.			
	Written sources – old birthday cards, gravestones, birth certificates, family letters	What do they tell us?			
Story	Family stories Local stories Stories about events in the past Famous people Eyewitness accounts Fiction Myth and legend	Oral Read, discuss, retell, rewrite, draw, act. Books Picture-stories Tapes Film Video Ballads & folk songs Plays Newspapers	1ab 2bc 3abc	1,2,3	

emphases to prevent rigidity or repetition. Table 3.1 gives some suggestions for linked starting points, activities and assessment. Year 1 and 2 children can present their findings, ultimately, for audiences within or beyond the school, as older children can, through slide shows, video or sound tapes, drama or role-play (developed from a home-corner reconstruction of an old kitchen , for example), story-telling, a museum exhibition, or 'stalls' presenting the researches of each group (maybe led by a parent or older visitor). They can display models and paintings or make up quizzes and games. Certainly, they can use word-processing for impressive collaborative writing, and use a simple data-base to record answers to their questionnaires. Teacher assessment, however, will need to be through talking to and observing children engaged in these activities at intervals over the whole project, because oral responses will be more detailed, more reflective and reveal more of their thinking strategies than is possible in writing. Labelled drawings and picture stories or stories with 'bubbles' could also be helpful.

The planning and implementation of key stage 2

Selecting the study units

Plan A

For the first time, content for the primary curriculum in history has been prescribed. It is essential that teachers do not become daunted by the number of study units they are expected to teach, and allow the curriculum to be content led. Many people were taught history as vast quantities of received knowledge to be memorised, regurgitated and forgotten without it having been made their own, without being involved in recognising and responding to its questions, its problems, its conflicts, its relevance, its dynamism. They were expected to cover so much ground that there was no time for the detail, for the local perspective, for discussion, argument, reflection, for the satisfaction of reaching a reasonable conclusion to an enquiry, or else the fascination of admitting that there is no one satisfactory answer. It is not surprising that most people's experience of the subject is boredom, or else a theme-park understanding that it may be entertaining but is superficial, not intellectually challenging or spiritually moving. How do we put together the required nine study units in a way that will not reawaken these sentiments, in ourselves, and in our pupils?

Table 3.2: *Key stage 2 – a local study*

Sources	Starting points	Activities	Assessment AT1	AT2	AT3
Maps	An important historical issue, linked to national trends involving either:	(a) Groups could research different buildings within the theme (e.g. either schools, churches, places connected with leisure), correlating findings on time-lines, through discussion, make display.	1a	2	1
Photos	(a) an aspect of local history		2abc	3	2
Pictures	e.g. education		3abc	4	3
Newspapers	leisure –		4abc	5	4
Parish records	(holiday resort)		5abc		5
Census returns	religion				
Gravestones	hospitals	(b) Time selected may be chosen for particularly rapid change (e.g. introduction of railway) or because of a particular event (e.g. outbreak of war) or a particular personality.			
Street directions	a local industry				
Local histories	(b) an aspect of local history over a short period of time				
Oral accounts					
Buildings		(c) Choice of unit illustrated would depend on resources in the locality e.g. a Roman fort or villa, Victorian building, Elizabethan house, or museum or gallery with a relevant collection (a railway, agricultural, canal, maritime museum).			
Artefacts					
	(c) an aspect of local history illustrating developments taught in another unit.				
Cross-referenced to analyse use of different sources, incompleteness, bias, conformatory and non-conformatory evidence.			Activities can be focused to reflect all the ATs across almost all the levels 2–5.		

Certainly, this should be a whole-staff operation, and, like history itself, should involve discussion, and argument for there is a vast range of equally valid solutions and people's personal interests and commitment are essential and must be taken into account. The following strategy seems logical. It could even be fun! Cut out cards in four colours (e.g. a pile of red, green, blue and white). On the red cards, write the titles of the core study units; mark the compulsory ones with a cross. On the blue cards, write the titles of the thematic units, on the green cards the titles of non-European units. Make two white cards each of which is a local study unit. Then draw up a board with rectangles (4 × 3) onto which the cards will fit. The columns represent terms 1–3 and the rows years 2–6. (Schools with a two-form entry could use separate boards, although there seem to be many advantages in year groups working together.) Vertically grouped classes across two years could reverse a two year sequence.

Move 1: the compulsory core study units It seems important to decide where to place these first.
Decisions to consider:

(a) Should they be chronological? There is no evidence that children learn a sense of time or chronology through learning about periods in sequence, and it seems likely that the reverse is true. There is no good reason to assume that earlier periods are more simple. If, however, you are convinced of the need for sequence, should the sequence go from the immediate past backwards or vice-versa? Decisions may be influenced by a school journey to an area with connections with a particular period.

(b) Are you going to choose Victorian Britain (CSU 3) or Britain since 1930 (CSU 4)? To choose both will mean doing two core units, which both seem worthy of a depth study in one year, and two history-focused terms may not be possible. The choice seems to depend on whether you would want to extend either the Victorians or Britain since 1930 as a local study, depending on the resources available within the locality. Alternatively, you may choose Britain since 1930 as a core study, because the buildings in the locality or the school was Victorian, and so cover both periods in this way.

(c) Exploration and encounters (CSU 6) is a compulsory unit; it seems possible to either superimpose it on the Tudors and Stuarts (CSU 2) rectangle, or to put it on one of the adjacent terms.

(d) If you do not decide to teach the units in chronological sequence, how are you to decide on the order? It may be that you decide to leapfrog (e.g. Greece, Britain since 1930, Invaders, Tudors and Stuarts), in

Grid for planning related History Study Units within an integrated curriculum order to challenge children's developing sense of chronology. It may be that there are resources in the locality which you think are better appreciated at a particular age, or that there are resources some distance away, which it would be better to travel to with older children. Teachers' interests are also an important consideration.

Move 2: thematic units (supplementary A) You only have to choose one of these.
Decisions to consider:

(a) Is the theme going to be linked with a science/technology focused theme? Any of the themes could be, but 'Domestic life' and 'Writing and printing' are possibly not so closely linked as the other themes. Does the colleague responsible for technology have a favourite historical theme?

(b) Does anyone else have a particular interest or expertise in science and technology which they would like to apply to history?

(c) Are there local resources to support one theme better – an area of continuous agricultural settlement or a farm visit as a starting point for Food and farming, a local interest in ships which links with Ships and seafarers, or a house or church to use as a focus for Houses and places of worship? Domestic life, families and childhood may be better resourced with artefacts related to Victorian Britain, or Britain since 1930. Is there a local museum with a particular speciality?

(d) What are the obvious or most interesting links between core units and themes (e.g. Tudors and Stuarts, with Exploration and encounters, and with Ships and seafarers, or Victorian Britain and Ships and seafarers, or Invaders and Ships and seafarers? Writing and printing and Tudors and Stuarts? Land transport and the Victorians?).

Having (tentatively) decided on which theme to choose, which core unit to link it to, and whether to use it to introduce or follow the core, place your chosen grey card on the board, adjacent to the related core study unit.

Move 3: Non-European study units You have to choose one of these.
Decisions to consider:

(a) Resources. The British Museum provides excellent teaching resources on Ancient Egypt, Mesopotamia and Assyria. The AKLOWA centre at Takely in Hertfordshire arranges activities (cooking, dancing, drumming, printing, pottery), which help children to learn about traditional West African life.

(b) The interests of the children. Children in the school may have interests in a particular area.

48

(c) Members of staff may have particular experience of an area, through their own study, or history, or travel.

(d) How can the non-European units be linked to core study units? Egypt and Greece for example, complement each other; this may or may not be a reason for doing both. Benin could be linked to Tudors and Stuarts or to Victorians.

(e) How do the non-European units link to geography units that may be planned?

(f) Are there links with religious education you would like to make?

Place your chosen green card next to the appropriate core unit.

Move 4: the local study (supplementary unit B) The position of this card also depends on resources and interests:

(a) Are there resources which relate particularly to core or thematic units chosen?

(b) Was there a period of particular interest or great change in the local community, or an issue or a person of particular interest?

(c) Is there a theme which is particularly relevant, for example leisure activities in a holiday town?

You can now place the white card on the board.

Move 5 You have laid 8 cards (if you combined CSU 2 and CSU 6). You can now choose any card you have previously rejected with reluctance, and place it wherever you like!

Move 6 If you opted for an integrated curriculum, superimpose science and geography-focused topics, which will link with the supplementary units chosen.

Plan B

An alternative approach which has been adopted by one school is for the whole school (Years 3–6) to work on the same core study unit for the central term each year. They began with the Victorians. This is an attractive idea because, firstly it enables teachers to share ideas and expertise, collect resources together and support each other, and secondly it emphasises the need to plan for and assess progression in thinking. To be sure that real progression is being achieved using different content is difficult. If the study unit throughout the key stage is the same for each year group, it is possible to monitor progression in a more precise way. On occasions, the entire seven to eleven age group could, for instance, be responding to the same piece of evidence.

Teachers will then need to look for ways of encouraging different levels of response.

Whichever plan is adopted a whole-school approach is essential. Where work of quality has been found (DES, 1989), it has been identified as dependent on documentation with clear aims, in terms of knowledge, skills and attitudes, produced through consultation, with advice on resources and how to plan first-hand experiences, and a consistent approach to planning and assessment throughout the school. Effective learning involved discussion and questioning, beginning with the children's existing knowledge, and introducing new facts and ideas, related to a series of focal points. Teachers showed children how to investigate primary sources to find out about the relationship between the past and the present, or what it might like to be someone else. Investigations were recorded in a variety of artistic, creative and mathematical forms.

CHAPTER 4

Case Studies: Plans and Examples of Work

In this chapter, four case studies will be described of work in history which was undertaken with classes throughout the five to eleven age-range, as part of an integrated curriculum. The work was done after the National Curriculum for the core subjects was introduced but prior to the Statutory Orders for history; it is therefore encouraging that it encompasses the attainment targets and appropriate Statements of Attainment in the core subjects and also in history. For each case study, there is a cross-curricular web showing how other disciplines are related to the history topic, although it was not intended that all work had to fit into the topic. Work in mathematics in particular was often extended, or a sub-theme introduced. The web is followed by a subject grid for history showing how planning is related to assessment. Similar grids were devised for each of the other curriculum areas. (It is important to stress that this work was planned for two classes. Not all the children did all the activities, and specific assessment tasks could be selected by the teacher or chosen by the pupil.) The grids are followed by diagrams showing how the work was organised around several focuses, over a term. Each section concludes with examples of children's work. These were typical, but were not chosen because of their particular interest; since samples were not kept at the time and children took their work home at the end of a term, it was difficult to collect work from previous years – a cautionary tale. The precise assessment levels shown in the grids were added after the projects took place, since this work preceded the National Curriculum. Therefore, the examples chosen do not reflect the range of learning outcomes as accurately as they could. In spite of the difficulty of interpreting the statements, it does seem likely that if the work had been planned with these clearly defined aims in mind, samples of work allowing more rigorous assessment, and displaying higher levels of historial thinking could have been achieved. Some examples were chosen because they

52

represented historical problem-solving. Others show how science, mathematics or language were related to the theme.

'Me' Year 2 – key stage 1 levels 1–3

Years 1 and 2 worked on the theme 'Me' with a history focus. Year 1 concentrated on their own time-lines for six years, which recorded their own experiences of change over time. They brought in their own baby clothes, and toys they had had over the previous five years, sequenced socks and mittens to illustrate growth, sequenced their photographs, and recounted memories. They interviewed one of the parents about a new baby who was brought into school, weighed, measured and compared with them. They listed their achievements since they were babies: talking, throwing and catching balls, and so on. The children were also paired with Year 6 children as part of the Year 6 work on 'human development'. Each pair worked on a cross-curricular theme planned by the older child for a week, at their own level. One pair, for instance, studied an old oil lamp, wrote about it, painted it and found out about it, each in their own way, then they put the resulting work in a book and discussed similarities and differences of the five-year-old ten-year-old approaches. Both the Year 1 and Year 6 children enjoyed this, and it enabled the younger children to predict what they may be like and able to do when they are 'twice as old as now'.

The Year 1 teacher and the head-teacher also participated 'at their own level'. The Year 1 teacher made her own time-line illustrated with photographs of her family and key events in her life, concluding with her Graduation Day and her wedding. Since she was *twenty-five*, this was a *very long* time-line, and allowed the children to discuss their life span in relation to hers, and to compare different scales for recording time. The teacher displayed her own collection of books and toys, surrounding her wedding dress on a stand in the middle of the room and invited her own grandma to come to school! Gran, teacher, and children, all enjoyed exchanging memories. Meanwhile, in the foyer, the headmistress, who was new to the school, took the opportunity both to introduce herself and to support the history project, by making her time-line. This was *very long indeed* because she was nearly fifty years old. She was able to show us photographs of her father leaving home to go to war and other very personal records – a long swathe of her golden hair, cut when she was five, her fifty-year-old teddy, her first mitten. She told us in one assembly, a moving story of how she had found these things hidden in a secret box in her parents home on

53

Diagram 4.1: Core study unit 1. Key stage 1

History

AT 1-5

1. *Time-lines*: sequencing and describing changes over time, related to personal experiences. — AT 1
2. *Class museum or house corner reconstruction*. How the past was different, from domestic artefacts. — AT 1 } 3
3. Visit to Museum of Childhood: finding out about the past through toys. — AT 2
4. *Oral history* — AT 3
5. *Local photographs* Visit identifying and describing change. — AT 1
6. *Stories*: local myths and legends. — AT 1 } 2

Geography
Identify, observe, talk about photos of familiar places.
Identify activities, use of land and buildings in locality.
Recognise adults do different kinds of work.
Understand homes are part of a locality, reasons why people made journeys, different forms of transport.
Describe ways in which people have changed environment.

Language

Listen to 'oral history' and ask questions.
Describe incidents in own life.
Discuss artefacts, photographs.
Listen to stories, ask questions.

Read pictures, stories, museum labels, birth certificates, shop and street names.
Make deductions.

Write questionnaires for parents, explanations for photos/artefacts, stories.

'Me'
A Term's Project with a history focus.

R.E.

1. Rules: were they the same/different in the past?
'Moral tales' from old Sunday school prizes, and story books today. Rules when granny was little, and now.
2. Places of worship in locality.
3. Myths, legends, stories.

Science/Technology

1. *Ourselves*. Keeping food fresh (then and now), Exercise/games (then and now). What are they made of? How do they work?
2. *Toys* old/new.
3. (a) *Make dolls' house* with lighting circuit, burglar alarm. Make furniture. Dolls' clothes (materials).
   (b) Sort domestic artefacts: old/new, similarities/differences.
4. Oral history – effects of technological changes on people's lives.

Art

1. Self portraits.
2. Finger prints → classifying and drawing.
3. Book-making.
4. Designing fabric and wallpapers for dolls' house.
5. Drawing old artefacts.
6. Pottery models of favourite foods/meals.

Maths

Time-line calculations
Mapping positions of dolls furniture

Family trees
Sets of toys old/new, materials, how they work
Probability – in predicting own life events

Diagram 4.2: 'Me' history grid

What I want children to learn	What I want the children to do	Assessment
To describe and explain historical change and cause	I Time-lines (a) Make own time-line 0–7 (i) Place photographs of themselves correctly (ii) Write questionnaire for parents about events in their (child's) life; put these on time-line (iii) Compare with similar time-line for teacher	AT 1 2 a) Can put events, photographs in chronological order c) Can identify differences 3 a) Can describe changes
To acquire evidence from historical sources	(b) Bring in 'old things' for house corner role-play, for class museum. Draw them; attach (by Velcro which allows rearrangement) to a sequence line with categories (very old/ old/new). Discuss sequence and adjust. (c) Visit to Museum of Childhood. Handling session – old toys. What were they made of? What are they? How did they work?	AT 1 2 a) c) 3 a) AT 3 1 Can explain what an artefact is 2 Can suggest how it works, how it was used. 3 Can suggest how it affected the lives of people who made/used it

Diagram 4.2: Cont

What I want children to learn	What I want the children to do	Assessment	
To understand interpretations of history	II *Oral history* (i) Write questionnaire for granny, grandad or older person about life when they were little or tape-record interview at home	AT 2 2	Can understand that different grannies/grandads spent the past in different ways
	(ii) Invite several older people who were brought up in different parts of the world and different circumstances to tell children about their early years, show photographs of themselves in the past, and their treasured possessions.	3	Can explain what is known for certain about the past from these accounts (possibly through books with photographs, or presentation for grandparents, or making tape or video recordings for 'children's radio or TV')
	III *Photographs* Collect and display selected old photographs of locality, take photographs of/visit same sites today.	AT 1 2 c)	Can identify changes
	IV *Story* (i) Invite someone from a local history society to tell 'true stories' about locality which children can retell, draw, act out.	AT 1 1 a) 2 b)	Can retell story Act it. Explain why people acted as they did
	(ii) Myths and legends from different cultures.	AT 2 1	Can explain how you know people really existed, or why you think they did not

Diagram 4.3: *Plan showing how work for the term was organised around four focuses, each lasting several weeks*

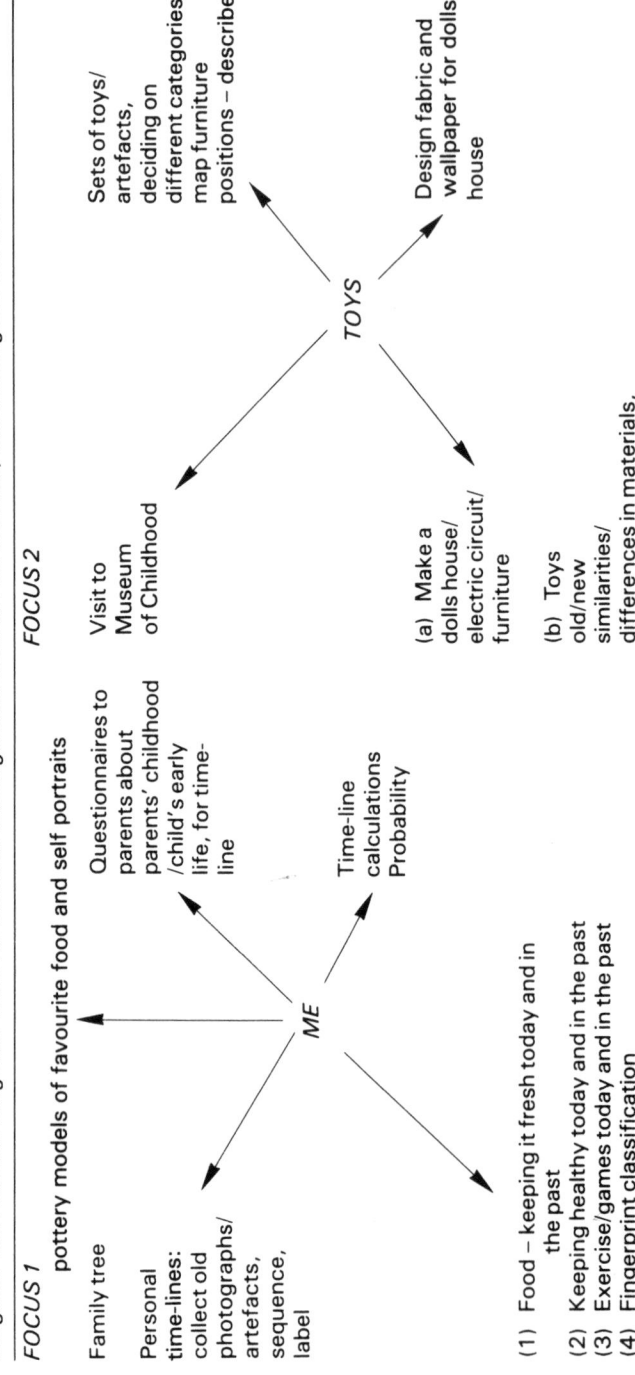

FOCUS 1

pottery models of favourite food and self portraits

Family tree

Personal time-lines: collect old photographs/ artefacts, sequence, label

FOCUS 2

Questionnaires to parents about parents' childhood /child's early life, for time-line

Time-line calculations
Probability

Visit to Museum of Childhood

(a) Make a dolls house/ electric circuit/ furniture

(b) Toys old/new similarities/ differences in materials, in how they work

TOYS

Sets of toys/ artefacts, deciding on different categories, map furniture positions – describe

Design fabric and wallpaper for dolls' house

ME

(1) Food – keeping it fresh today and in the past
(2) Keeping healthy today and in the past
(3) Exercise/games today and in the past
(4) Fingerprint classification
(5) The senses: smelling, tasting

Diagram 4.3: Cont

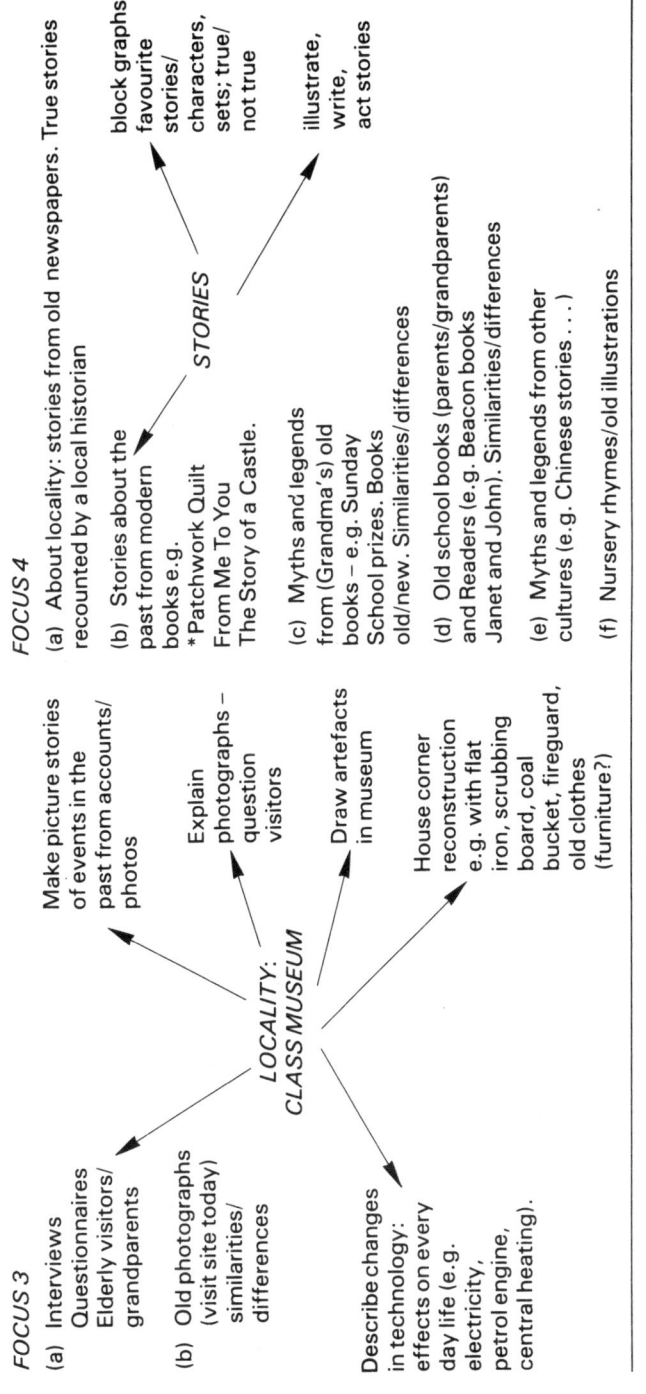

FOCUS 3

(a) Interviews
Questionnaires
Elderly visitors/
grandparents

(b) Old photographs
(visit site today)
similarities/
differences

Describe changes
in technology:
effects on every
day life (e.g.
electricity,
petrol engine,
central heating).

Make picture stories
of events in the
past from accounts/
photos

Explain
photographs –
question
visitors

Draw artefacts
in museum

House corner
reconstruction
e.g. with flat
iron, scrubbing
board, coal
bucket, fireguard,
old clothes
(furniture?)

LOCALITY:
CLASS MUSEUM

FOCUS 4

(a) About locality: stories from old newspapers. True stories
recounted by a local historian

(b) Stories about the
past from modern
books e.g.
*Patchwork Quilt
From Me To You
The Story of a Castle.

STORIES

(c) Myths and legends
from (Grandma's) old
books – e.g. Sunday
School prizes. Books
old/new. Similarities/differences

(d) Old school books (parents/grandparents)
and Readers (e.g. Beacon books
Janet and John). Similarities/differences

(e) Myths and legends from other
cultures (e.g. Chinese stories . . .)

(f) Nursery rhymes/old illustrations

block graphs:
favourite
stories/
characters,
sets; true/
not true

illustrate,
write,
act stories

Note: * *The Patchwork Quilt* Valerie Flournoy. Puffin. 1987.
From Me To You. Paul Rogers. Orchard Books. 1987.
The Story of a Castle John S. Goodall. Andre Deutsch. 1986.

their death. In other assemblies, she read to us moral tales from her parents' Sunday school prizes. This infant project developed excellent inter-personal understandings and insights throughout the whole-school community, at far more than ten levels!

The Year 2 extension of the theme was originally going to be 'when Granny was little', but since grannies ranged in age from mid-thirties to about sixty, this was not a very useful title, and certainly did not go back to pre-electricity, and horse-drawn carts. So they stuck to an extended version of 'me'. This was not a multi-cultural school, but a Chinese boy had recently joined the class. He spoke little English and did not adjust easily. The class teacher seized this opportunity to develop his work on 'when Mummy was little' into a rich sub-theme on what it was like to grow up in Shanghai, with the help of the boy's mother. The class went to the Chinese exhibition, and went to see the Chinese New Year festivities in Soho. This led to work on old Chinese tales, with big collages and models of dragons and of the 'Willow Pattern Plate', work on Chinese paintings, experiments in writing with a Chinese brush in ink, and Chinese calendars and counting systems. The term concluded with a Chinese meal which Mrs Chan showed the children how to prepare, then they compared old China with what Mrs Chan told them about life in China today, and how life in Shanghai is different from and similar to life in Croydon! The Chinese work gave the project a far richer dimension and also led to greater personal understandings for all those involved. ALO–WA (1990) a book of stories, memories, and photographs written by a black women's oral history group at the Willowbank Urban Studies Centre in Southwark is another example of how rich a starting point family and oral history can be.

Children's work

Some children's questionnaires for their parents ask about the arrival of cats, dogs, goldfish, brothers and sisters, about holidays, cuts and bruises, or moving home. This six-year-old however, is already preoccupied with self-assessment and monitoring her progress!

The information from the questionnaire was transferred to the time-line. There were great opportunities here for transactional writing and for parental involvement. Parental understanding and support is particularly important in family history which can be a sensitive area. The family tree was optional, and done with help at home.

The children were very interested to use the information in their

1 When did I First have our First tooth?
  I had my First tooth at five months old
2 When did I first walk?
  I first walked at 9 months

3 When did I first dress our selves?
  I first dressed at 18 months
4 When did I first read a book?
  When I was 4 years old

5 When did I first draw?
  When I was two years old
6 When did I start to write?
  I started to write when I was 4 years

7 When did I have money?
  When I was 3 years old

8 When did I know my numbers?
  I knew my numbers when I was 4 years

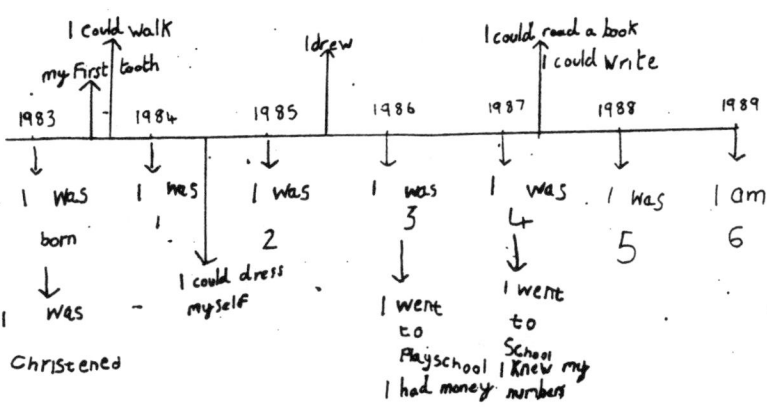

Gemma's family

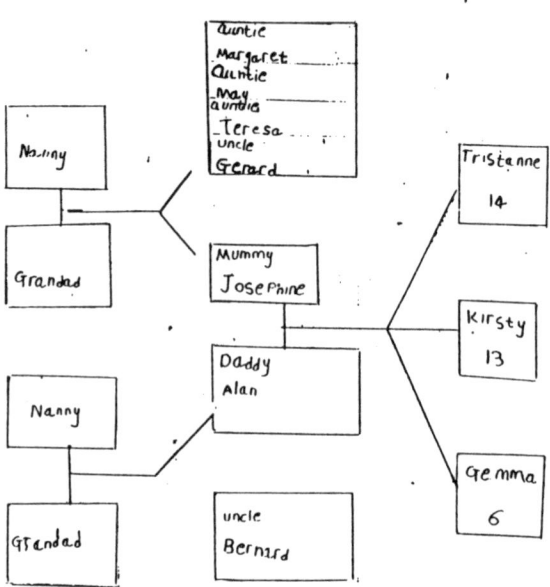

time-lines, photographs and collections of toys to make deductions about the past, and about changes over time. These were certainly 'interactive' displays.

mrs wiltshire dosh t play
with her tds she nsed
(used)
to go tap dancing and she hab
(d)
a typewritr her sisters name
was marilyn 1963 she was a
tiny little baby she grew
as she got older her nme
was sharon

OUR TRIP TO BETHNAL GREEN
TOY MUSEUM.

On Wednesday, 14th June, we went on the coach to the toy museum.
The coach driver took us to the wrong museum. We had to go on the underground When we got to the toy museum James had a nosebleed.
In the museum we saw old toys: Trains, cars, dolls, games, soldiers, puppets, doll's houses, boats, teddy bears, horses and theatres.
We found out that old toys were made from wood and our new toys are made from plastic. WE found out that dolls were made out of wood, wax, china, clay, paper and plastic. lots of old dolls had real hair.
We had a talk about old toys—it was very interesting.
We were tired when we got home.

A Story by Class 7.

Gemma

Toys

our grandprents would

have played with

hoops and ropes

dolls

Doll were made out of clay and wax wood and paper and china and we saw tooth brush dolls and we saw a plug face and we saw Queen Victoria and the dolls hair was real and our dolls don t have real hair and we saw toy town

The account of the visit to the Museum of Childhood is a piece of shared writing. It refers, in a very sanguine way, to the initial excitement of the day, when the coach driver deposited the children outside Burlington Arcade, telling the teacher, 'It's just up the road love' (assuming they were going to the Museum of Mankind!). Although she had made a preliminary visit, the teacher assumed that this was another entrance. The novelty of the tube journey from Piccadilly Circus to Bethnal Green was so exciting that James had a nosebleed before they were able to discuss such concepts as continuity and change, similarity and difference, during the 'handling session' led by the museum staff. Later, they wrote a book explaining how the toys in the past were sometimes different from theirs, and why.

Ancient Greece Years 5–6 – key stage 2 core study unit 5

Years 5 and 6 worked together on this project, in a shared 'open plan' area. It began with children deciding to set up a travel agency in a corner of the room, in order to find out what Greece is like today. Eleven-year-olds, boys and girls, often enjoy the excuse for this sort of role-play. They collected brochures, time-tables and posters from local travel agents, made and displayed their own information sheets, booklets and booking forms, and enclosed the corner behind net curtains suspended from the ceiling. They set up a reception area with easy chairs, installed a computer, telephones (unconnected) and coffee-making facilities! Their efficiency compared favourably with the shop in the High Street. Having planned their holidays, everyone made themselves an effective passport (photocopying the front of a passport on to yellow paper and sticking this on to black card, with their school photograph inside) and filled in a booking form. The booking form involved complex calculations of time, speed and distance, money, and also of weight; a collection of possible luggage items was made in a suitcase, ranging from snorkels and sun cream to 'evening wear', which was weighed so that suitable choices within the luggage allowance could be made. Later in the term, one group used the information they had acquired to make a video tape of a 'Travel Programme' about Greece. Groups also took it in turns to cook a Greek lunch once a week, with the help of a parent, and invited a chosen guest. (It was a school tradition to cook a meal on the theme of the class project.)

The travel agency led into the second focus, finding out about changes within Ancient Greek civilisation, by making a time-line, supported by maps, showing key events, people and architecture. The study unit (giving an overview of the period) was introduced through class lessons, describing and explaining the broad historical canvas. This was a useful exercise in note-taking. The notes were then used to make individual time-lines.

The children learned a great deal of mathematics in making their models of Greek temples. This involved choosing a photograph of a particular temple, finding out or estimating its dimensions, reducing these to one hundredth the actual size, then drawing the nets to make the model: a series of cuboids for the steps, cylinders for the pillars, a triangular prism for the roof or portico. They then had to describe their model using listed concepts: angles, edges, faces, height, length, area. This is a useful mathematics assessment exercise because the models varied in complexity, and so did the descriptions, from 'my model has twenty-four right angles' to 'the area of the right angle triangles forming the end faces of the triangle-based prism is 50 sq.cm'. Number patterns attributed to Pythagoras were a useful entry into triangle and square numbers and Pythagoras theorem. Learning about and using the Greek counting system was also a good way of testing children's understanding of place value. One child told us that this reminded him of the 'golden rectangle'. Since the teacher was not knowledgeable on this subject, he brought in his book and explained it to everyone!

The third focus was on myths and legends. This was related to music-making in Ancient Greece, a convenient way of integrating the science attainment target on sound, which the whole school had decided to tackle. The British Museum leaflet on Greek musical instruments was an excellent introduction to Ancient Greek stringed and wind instruments, which, we learned, might accompany recited poetry. First, children experimented to discover the variables influencing pitch, then they each designed and constructed an instrument on which a series of four notes of different pitch could be played. This produced an ingenious variety of solutions. They then wrote poems based on stories in the *Odyssey* to be accompanied on their instrument! One group decided to make a tape-recording of a programme for schools explaining how they had done this, before recording their poem.

Another addition to the theme was the news that Derek Walcott, the West Indian poet, had been awarded the W.H. Smith Literary Award for his poem *Omeros*, which transposes the Homer stories of Hector, Achilles and the fought-over Helen to a fishing community in St Lucia. It also includes a dream-like fantasy of a West Indian wandering in exile in Europe and the story of Philoctetes, a yam-keeper with a 'symbolic wound' inherited from the 'chained ankles of his grandfather'. It cannot be pretended that we read all 325 pages, but the story did offer an unexpected multicultural dimension to Homer, as Walcott puts it, transported, 'across centuries of the sea's parchment atlas'. A PGCE student working in a multicultural school, subsequently achieved some wonderful poetry from Year 6 children with Greek, Turkish and Caribbean backgrounds, after reading them Leon Garfield's version of the Prometheus story in *The God Beneath the Sea*.

The fourth focus was based on a visit to the British Museum. Each group of three or four children chose a particular showcase in Room

69 to study, drawing artefacts and taking notes from labels, in order to find out about different aspects of life in Ancient Greece. In school, they then designed and made an impressive museum, raised on staging blocks, with a facade from floor to ceiling consisting of pillars made from rolls of corrugated card painted grey, supporting a pediment decorated by enlarging photocopies of motifs from a Greek frieze. The exhibits, labelled and explained in the brochure, were mainly drawings of artefacts seen in the British Museum, replica pottery, some modern Greek holiday souvenirs, and large posters made by projecting slides of pictures on Greek vases and copying the image accurately. These were used as evidence exercises, as in 'The Hoplite Race' quoted in the examples of work.

An interesting opportunity occurred for the children to extend the teachers' plans in an unexpectedly successful way, towards the end of term. They had been watching a television programme about archaeology in Greece. Prompted by this, one group asked if they could see what they could find in the rough area of school grounds. Not expecting them to find anything of interest, the teacher suggested they mark off a square metre, and dig for twenty minutes. The results, in an area which had previously been allotments, proved so exciting that a number of other groups ended up undertaking a systematic excavation, which revealed broken pottery, a variety of old bottles (from Victorian to HP Sauce), clay pipes, parts of tools, plumbing, and old shoes. When they unearthed a tractor tyre and the beginning of some steps, they decided 'there may have been a farm house here'. Someone decided to go to the local library for further information; someone else sought out people who had lived in the area for some time, to question them. The children spontaneously decided to make a scale plan of the 'site' where the artefacts had been found. These were carefully measured and drawn, and put on a time-line in estimated sequence, in order to guess what they might tell us about the site before the school was built. The children did most of this in their spare time, no tetanus jabs were required, and it proved an excellent way of evaluating the historical thinking processes they had learned and were able to transfer.

Finally, it seems important to stress that neither of the teachers had any specialist knowledge of Ancient Greece, and since the project took place in the Spring term after a very short Christmas break, they had little preparation time. Their own initial reading was limited to a selection of children's books from the local library, and to *The Times Atlas of Ancient Civilizations* (1989). It is salutary that teachers do not

Diagram 4.4: *Core study unit 5. Key stage 2 – Ancient Greece*

Maths

(a) *Set up travel agency* — AT 1/9 +
  (i) Plan, book and cost holiday
  (ii) Luggage allowance — AT 8
  (iii) Route. Journey times. — 11
(b) *Make model of chosen* — AT 2
  Greek temple (nets, scale, — 8
  properties of cylinders, — 10
  cuboids, prisms).
(c) Pythagoras ∆ numbers — AT 5
  ▢ numbers — 6
  theorem
  golden rectangle
(d) *Olympic Games* — AT 8
  (BM notes).
  Measuring speed, distance,
  variables affecting projectiles.
(e) Time-line (scale, measure).

English — AT 1/2

(a) Stories from *Odyssey*, legends, myths, contemporary accounts.
(b) Debate the role of women in Ancient Greece. — AT 3
(c) Explanations: science experiments; deductions from evidence.
(d) Travel programme video.
(e) Notes and reference work.
(f) Museum brochure.
(g) Travel agents literature.
(h) Stories – explain constellations then and now.
(i) Poetry writing.

Science/Technology — AT 1/2

(a) Sound (Pythagoras)
  (i) Find out about Greek musical instruments (BM teachers' notes)
  (ii) Experiments to discover variables influencing pitch (length, thickness, tautness)
  (iii) Design and make your own instrument which plays 4 notes in sequence
  (iv) Pythagoras' discovery of relationship between length, vibration and pitch.
(b) Volume experiments (Archimedes). — AT 3
(c) Space. Constellations – (Greek myths). Plot positions of stars on grids.

Art — AT 14

(a) Drawings from Greek vases (for evidence exercise and museum).
(b) Screen printing – Greek motifs.
(c) Postcards (from 'Greek' holiday).
(d) Posters for Travel Agent.
(e) Wall painting. The Trojan Horse (true or false?).
(f) Greek Museum (+ design and technology).

History — AT 1

(a) *Time-line 1600BC–0* Class lessons, secondary sources to mark 4 periods and key events, people. — 3 abc, 4 abc, 5 abc
(b) *The Fall of Troy* Read about excavations and stories from the *Odyssey*. — AT 2, 1–5
(c) *Visit British Museum* Find out in groups about variety of aspects of Greek life. Draw artefacts and note information. — AT 3, 1–5
  Set up class museum and/or make travel brochure explaining what artefacts tell us about Ancient Greece.
(d) *Interpretations.* Pictures from later periods portraying

Geography

Set up travel agency.
Make travel programme.
Find out where Greece is and what it is like: maps – towns, relief; climate.
How do people live – food.
How do you get there?
How long does it take?
Maps of Europe, Greece, Mediterranean, Asia, in ancient times.

Music — AT 1 2 3 4 5

(a) Write 'music' to accompany your *Odyssey* poem, using own musical symbols.
(b) Play it.
(c) Make tape explaining how to do this for other groups of children.

R.E.

Myths
What questions did people in Ancient Greece ask, and how did they answer them?

Diagram 4.5: *Ancient Greece history grid*

What I want children to learn	What I want children to do	Assessment
AT 1	(i) Make time-line 1600BC–0. Mark 4 periods, key events, people, architecture.	
2 (c) Identify differences between past and present times	1600–1150BC Mycenean	2c Can make sets of 'Ancient Greek' and not 'Ancient Greek' things
3 (a) Describe changes over period of time	1000–479BC Expansion 478–405BC Golden Age 336–30BC Hellenistic	3a Can describe to an audience changes indicated by time-line
(b) Give reason for a historical event or development	(ii) Find out about each period. Write notes	
(c) Identify differences between times in the past	e.g. Mycenean metal work Mycenean beehive tombs Mycenean writings; fall of Mycenae	3b Can explain, as one of Xerxes soldiers why you were defeated
4 (a) Recognise that over time, some things changed and others stayed the same	→ Greek emigration to Asia Minor, Black Sea, Africa, trade city states, farming, Persian wars, and victory of Athens	
(b) Show awareness that historical events usually have more than one cause and consequence		
(c) Describe different feature of life of a historical period	→ Greek temples, Athenian democracy, theatres, Socrates, war between Athens and Sparta	4c Can describe different aspects of one of these periods (in groups) from information collected
5 (c) Show how different features in a historical situation relate to each other	→ Alexander the Great – Empire in N. Africa and Asia Greek medicine, mathematics and science Olympic Games, theatre	5c Can identify 'military' events (fall of Mycenae, defeat of Persia, defeat of Athens, Alexander's empire), and say how they caused other changes described by time-line in each period
	(iii) Draw maps to illustrate changes, making significant places, dates, routes	

During 1992, the intended meaning of AT2 became clarified through projects initiated by the National Curriculum Council (described in *Teaching History*, 72 (1993)). The general requirements for a programme of study (DES 1991, p. 16) state that pupils should have opportunities to develop awareness of different ways of representing past events, to investigate differences between versions of past events, and to examine reasons why versions of the past differ. AT2 is therefore seen as essentially concerned with accounts or reconstructions of a period in the past made at a subsequent time. These may be of varying status. 'It could include a theme park, a reconstruction of a civil war battle or an IT simulation... Alternatively, children can compare their own accounts of the past based on a selection of sources.' (Sue Bennett, professional officer for history at the National Curriculum Council, *Times Educational Supplement*, p. 43, December 1991). The behaviour, ideas and attitudes of different individuals or groups alive at the time are seen to be concerned with motive and therefore belong to AT1 strand c. Different interpretations of sources belong in AT3. For these reasons, planning suggestions for AT2 are different from those given in the first printing of this book.

Diagram 4.5: *Cont.*

What I want children to learn	What I want children to do	Assessment
AT 2		
2 Show awareness that different stories about the past can give different versions of what happened.	(i) Become aware of different ways of representing the past by collecting pictures of children in Ancient Greece (e.g. *Asterix at the Olympic Games* (1966). Goscinny and Uderzo. Dargaud Ed. Paris; *Ancient Lands and Peoples. Story and Play – Way Histories* p. 75 (c. 1940) F.E. West; Arnold; enlarged photocopies of pictures from other (old) children's books.	2 Can talk about differences between the pictures (how people are dressed, what they are doing, background details, mood, style of drawing) and consider when and why the pictures were made.
3 Distinguish between a fact and a point of view.	(ii) Read Stories from the *Odyssey*	3 *Odyssey*; True or False? Divide paper into two columns and list factual and legendary evidence.

Diagram 4.5: *Cont.*

What I want children to learn	What I want children to do	Assessment
4 Show understanding that deficiencies in evidence may lead to different interpretations of the past.	(iii) List questions that they would like to ask a child in Ancient Greece if it were possible.	4 Can highlight the questions which no-one today could answer with certainty.
5 Recognise that interpretations of the past may differ from what is known to have happened.	(iv) Pretend they are historians filling in a 'research sheet'. Collect images of children in Ancient Greece which were made at the time (e.g. vase paintings on post-cards or in books). Complete 'research sheet'.	5 'Research sheet' is divided into 2 columns headed 'the same' and 'different'. Can list similarities and differences between a contemporary and a subsequent picture.

AT 3

2. Recognise that historical sources can stimulate and answer questions about the past.	Visit to British Museum (Room 69). In small groups study a particular showcase of artefacts relating to one aspect of life in Ancient Greece. Draw and note given information	2 Can write descriptive labels of artefacts
3. Make deductions from historical sources	Display drawings (and postcards and clay models) in a 'class museum'. Write labels explaining what they tell us about life in Ancient Greece	3 Can explain what the artefacts tell us about Ancient Greece
4. Put together information from different historical sources		4 Can write a brochure for Museum or for tourists to Greece, using variety of sources
5. Comment on the usefulness of a historical source for a particular enquiry		5 Can explain, in brochure or in a presentation the usefulness of sources used

Diagram 4.6: *Plan showing how work for the term was organised around four focuses*

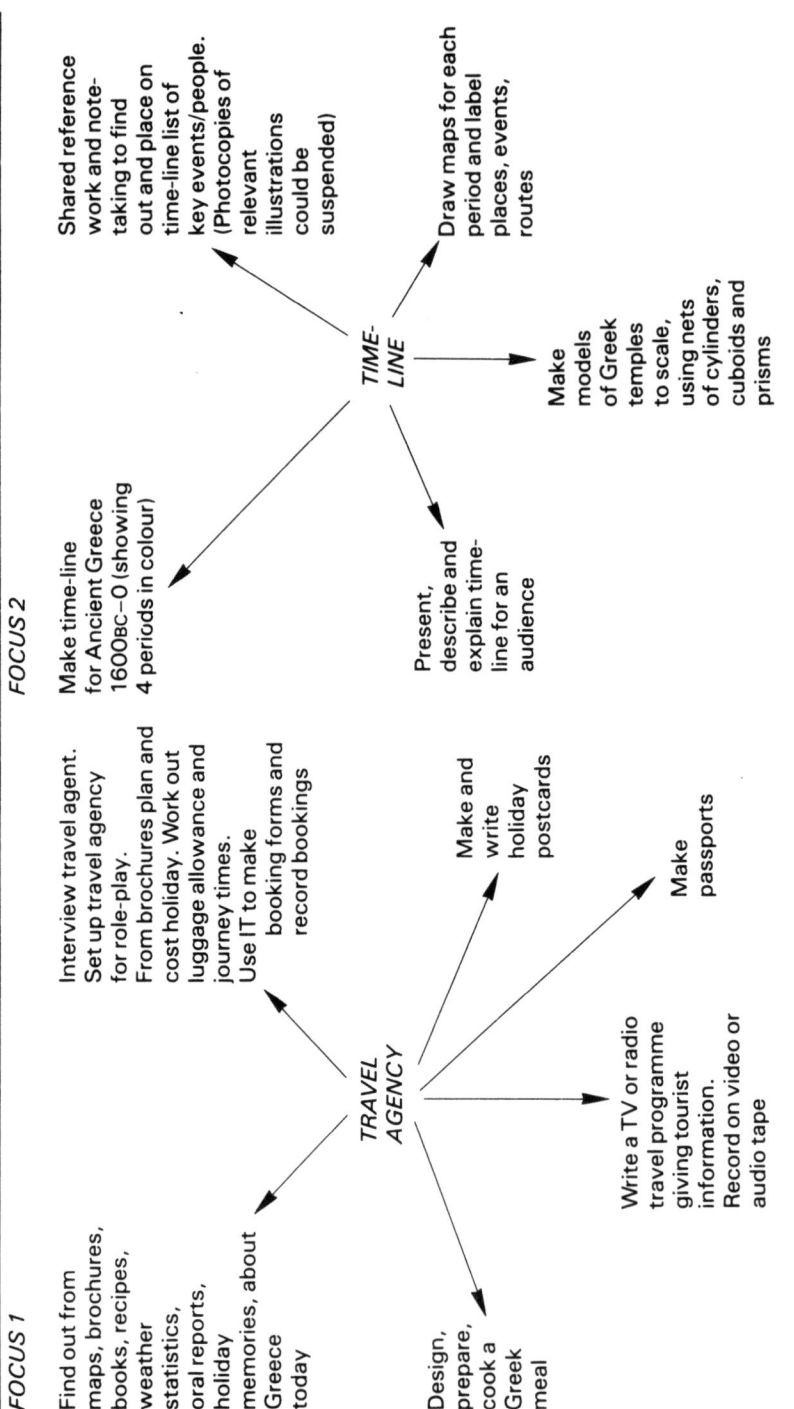

FOCUS 1

Find out from maps, brochures, books, recipes, weather statistics, oral reports, holiday memories, about Greece today

Design, prepare, cook a Greek meal

FOCUS 2

Make time-line for Ancient Greece 1600BC–0 (showing 4 periods in colour)

Interview travel agent. Set up travel agency for role-play.
From brochures plan and cost holiday. Work out luggage allowance and journey times.
Use IT to make booking forms and record bookings

TRAVEL AGENCY

Write a TV or radio travel programme giving tourist information. Record on video or audio tape

Make and write holiday postcards

Make passports

TIME-LINE

Shared reference work and note-taking to find out and place on time-line list of key events/people. (Photocopies of relevant illustrations could be suspended)

Draw maps for each period and label places, events, routes

Make models of Greek temples to scale, using nets of cylinders, cuboids and prisms

Present, describe and explain time-line for an audience

Diagram 4.6: *Cont*

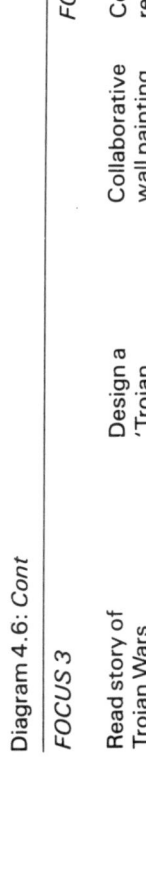

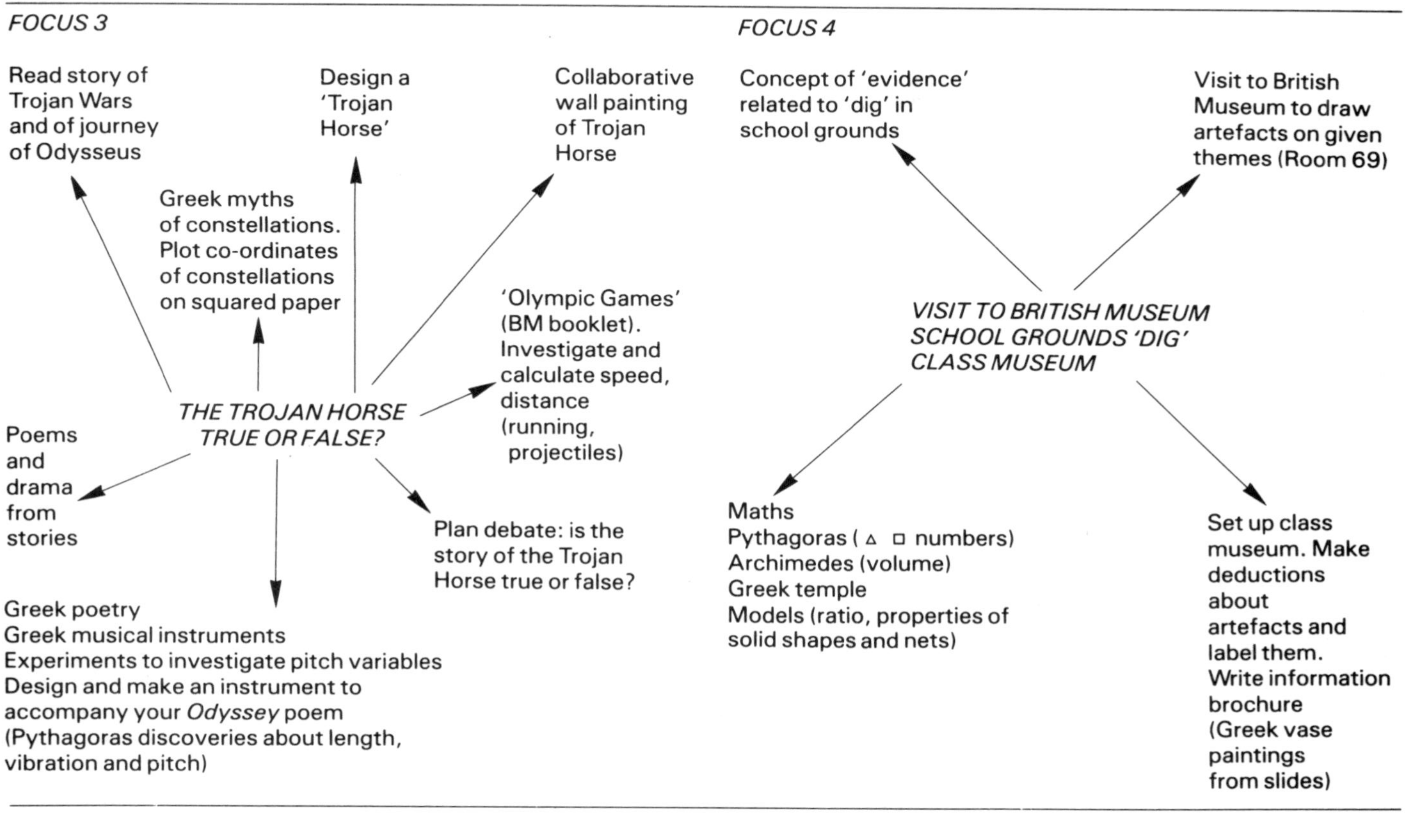

FOCUS 3

Read story of Trojan Wars and of journey of Odysseus

Design a 'Trojan Horse'

Greek myths of constellations. Plot co-ordinates of constellations on squared paper

Collaborative wall painting of Trojan Horse

'Olympic Games' (BM booklet). Investigate and calculate speed, distance (running, projectiles)

Plan debate: is the story of the Trojan Horse true or false?

THE TROJAN HORSE TRUE OR FALSE?

Poems and drama from stories

Greek poetry
Greek musical instruments
Experiments to investigate pitch variables
Design and make an instrument to accompany your *Odyssey* poem (Pythagoras discoveries about length, vibration and pitch)

FOCUS 4

Visit to British Museum to draw artefacts on given themes (Room 69)

Concept of 'evidence' related to 'dig' in school grounds

VISIT TO BRITISH MUSEUM SCHOOL GROUNDS 'DIG' CLASS MUSEUM

Set up class museum. Make deductions about artefacts and label them. Write information brochure (Greek vase paintings from slides)

Maths
Pythagoras (△ ☐ numbers)
Archimedes (volume)
Greek temple
Models (ratio, properties of solid shapes and nets)

72

need to feel inadequate if they do not have specialist knowledge of a period as long as they are prepared to share the excitement of the learning process. This is probably of greater educational value. (However, we were told that 'The Golden Age of Greece' is a Victorian idea, no longer held by historians!)

BOOKING FORM

Travellers Katie Snowden, Susan Hailstones

Destination Cyprus Paphos

Accomodation The Annabelle four star hotel

Transport British airways 757

Distance 3600 km

Departure time 17.45

Arrival time 23.59

Duration of Journey 6hr 14mins -2hr = 4hr 14mins

Speed 580 K.ph

Date of departure Monday 11th June

Luggage weight luggage allowance 20 Kgs

Cost per person £709 + £322 + £217 = £1248

Car Hire Metro £1550 x 14 = 217

Insurance £75

Children's work

Filling in the holiday booking form designed by the travel agency involved collaborative calculations: reading time-tables, the twenty-four hour clock, understanding time zones, ratio and distances, reading calendars, weight and money calculations involving large numbers, approximation, and the four rules of number.

The Hoplite Race

On our wall we have a painting of a Greek vase. The picture on the vase shows 'The Hoplite Race', one of the races in the Greek Olympic games.

What We Know For Certain

They carried their shields ∴ they were very strong. They raced naked and did not wear any shoes. They wore their helmits and their shields were half as big as they were. Two shields are the same so they were on the same side. They were men

What Reasnable Guesses can we make

It might have been at the begining of the race because the runners are close together. It might be a race with just 4 people because there is 4 people on our picture. It might have been a relay because they might use their shields for batons. It might be a training sesion. Maybee they did not really wear their helmits and carried. Carry their shields. Maybee

Large, carefully observed white on black paintings taken from projected slides of pictures on Greek vases decorated the class museum and were a basis for discussion of what they might tell us about Ancient Greece.

The British Museum booklet on the role of women in Ancient Greece, which contained quotations from contemporary male and female writers, seemed a good subject for discussion. This child's writing, however, shows how difficult it is to make a distinction between attitudes and values today and in the past, and the reasons

74

The bloke who did the painting put than in to show they were knights. Perhaps they carried these shields to test thier strength.

<u>What I would like to know.</u>

I would like to know why did they not wear any clothes? Was it a relay? Why did they have thier wepons? How tall and how old were the athletes? Were they married? Why was it painted in black and white?

why they may be different. Maybe the issue was too complex or the discussion not sufficiently structured by the teacher. Nevertheless, there is an incipient understanding that life in Ancient Greece was different. The child has applied her knowledge from another source that women had no political voice, then used this as a yard stick against society today, both in Britain and in other places. Although the ideas seem incoherent, there is evidence of reasoning, of recognising that the past was different, and yet some issues remain similar.

The huge mural of the Trojan Horse which the children painted dominated the 'book corner' and was a suitable background for reading Greek myths and legends. The children attempted to make a distinction between what was probably true and what was legend. This example shows that it is not difficult to suggest what is 'false' supported by a reason, because . . ., or but . . . . True aspects are more difficult to define or justify, because both supporting evidence and the child's knowledge of it is very limited.

A British Museum pamphlet introduced work on Greek musical instruments. This was followed by a science investigation to discover the variables influencing pitch. Children then designed and made their own 'instruments', which would play a sequence of four notes of different pitch. There was a rich variety of designs involving pipes or rubber bands. These were used to accompany poems based on the *Odyssey* stories. The Whirlpool was one such poem. Music was written using non-standard symbols. The description of the Golden Rectangle was discovered in a book at home by a child who demonstrated it in school for the benefit of the class and the teacher.

My thoughts

I disagree about women are wretched and have to be their husbands slave. Why cap'nt women go were ewhere they like with out asb. asking thar husbands. Most women in the UK don't go to work but stay home to clean and look after children Most of the men in the UK rown only see there children in the early morning and late evening.

Then again in anient Greece pealpe might think diffrently because the whole world was different then. The anicent Greeks propally had no say in the matter which is a big problem in todays parliament. There are still only a few women in parliament. But in ancient Greece women never voted. There are still place's in the world were this is true.

> Surely, of all creatures that have life and will, we women
> Are the most wretched. When for an extravagant sum,
> We have bought a husband, we must then accept him as
> Possessor of our body. This is to aggravate
> Wrong with worse wrong. Then the great question:
> will the man
> We get be bad or good? For women, divorce is not
> Respectable; to repel the man, not possible.

Euripides, Medea

76

Odyssey, True or False?

True	False.
I think there was a prinsess that was captured but I am not so.shure. sure shore that she was called Helen.	I do not think that there was a wooden horse because how could they have made it so big in a day.
I think there was a battle but I don't.know. think it hapened like the Odyssey says.	I do not belive a word of the Cyclops story for I do not believe in giants.
I think there was a woman called Circe.	I do not believe that Circe turned the men .it. into pigs but she might have cast a spell on them
I believe the syrans exsisted and sang thier songs.	I do not think that scylla the six headed mostor exsisted but I do think there was a whirlpool.
I think that Ulysses wife was called penahope.	✓

<u>Science investigation. - Sound.</u>

<u>What we wanted to find out.</u>

We wanted to find out how we could change the note of a string.

<u>What we did.</u>

First we put an elastic band round a cup a plucked it, to make a sound. First we changed the thickness of the band. The thicker band made a lower sound. Then we changed the tightness of the band. The Tighter band made a higher sound. Then we Put a pencil under the cub cup. The pencil changed the sound to a lower sound.

<u>Conclusion.</u>

We found out that you could change the note of a band by a) Thickening the band b) Change the tightness of the band c) putting an a pencil under the cup.

How we made a string Instrument.

Task.

What we had to do was to make a string Instrument with notes tuned to a musical scale. [!]

of different pitch.

What we did.

first we got a piece of wood and we banged 3 nails in. (A,B and C.) Then we got 'string J' and tied one end to 'nail A'. We then banged in nails D and G and wound string J round nail D and fastened it to nail G. We then did the same with the other 2 strings (K and L) and it finished off like this:

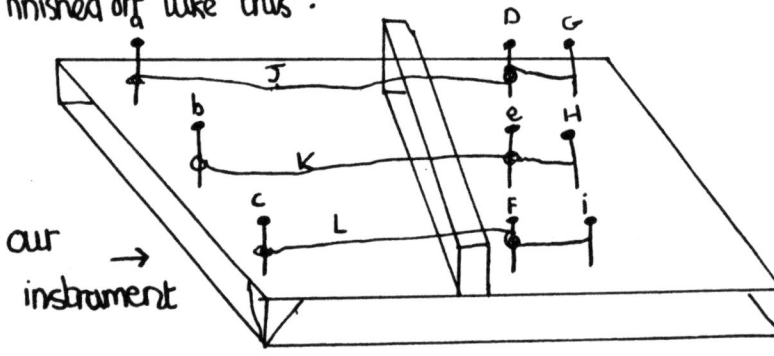

our → instrament

6

The Whirlpool,

Verse 1.

Between two rocks, near Syran island,
lies the whirlpool,
Water twisting,
Swirling, whirling, foam unfurling,
Sucking ships into its vortex.

Verse 2.

Six headed Scylla hungrily waits,
In her cave,
Suddenly moving;
Swirling, whirling, foam unfurling,
Swallowing men on passing ships.

Verse 3.

Ulysses ship sailed near the rocks,
survived the whirlpool,
faced the monster,
Swirling, whirling, foam unfurling,
Scylla ate 6 men - then safety.

The Golden Rectangle.

The construction of a Golden Rectangle begins with a square (shaded). Which is divided into two parts, by the line E to F. This (Point F) is the centre of a circle whose radius is the diagonal line F to C. An arc of the circle is drawn (C to G) and the base line (A to D) is extended to join with it. This becomes the base of the rectangle. The new side (H to G) is now drawn at right angles to the new base, and the line is brought out to meet it. The ratio between the sides in a golden rectangle is 1:1.6. The golden rectangle is a satisfying shape for a building.

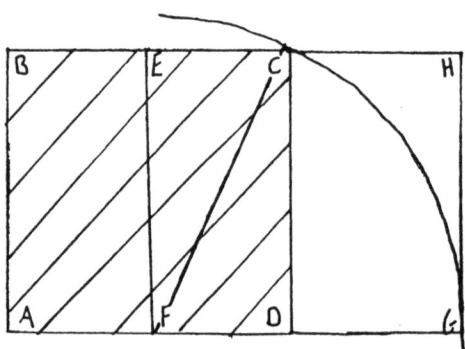

Tudor and Stuart times Year 5–6 – key stage 2 core study unit 2

Although in the National Curriculum Tudor and Stuart times constitutes one study unit, in these case studies, the Tudors and the Stuarts were taught as separate topics, each lasting a term, to different pairs of classes of Year 5 and Year 6 children. In the Tudor unit, after the initial overview of the period, describing key events and locating them on a time-line, there were two focuses, one on houses and one on ships. The teachers used one basic resource, the Elizabethan Age (Speed and Speed, 1987), supplemented by materials provided on visits to Hampton Court and to the Mary Rose. In the Stuart unit, there were four focuses, the Civil War, the Fire of London, Superstition and Beliefs, and 'the visit'. The last focus involved a choice of visit to either the Geffrye Museum, the National Portrait Gallery, or the Museum of London. The basic resource book used by the teachers in this unit was *The Seventeenth Century* by Paul Noble (1986), together with excellent materials from the museums and the Portrait Gallery.

In attempting to select from these focuses, it is important to define the essential threads which lie at the heart of the Tudor and Stuart period; the changing relationship between Church and State and the new social structure which was precipitated by this. Henry VIII established his position at the head of a church and a nation state which were not subject to the laws of the Roman Catholic Church in Rome. In order to defend it, he created the beginnings of British sea power. Exploration led to an increase in trade, and so the emergence of a powerful new class of merchants and 'gentry'. They were represented in parliament during the reign of Elizabeth I where they constantly challenged the authority of the Crown, a challenge Charles I was finally unable to resist. The break with Rome left a residue of loyal Roman Catholics in England, and also unleashed a spirit of independence in which a variety of beliefs flourished which were not encompassed either by Rome or by the Church of England. Thus the authority of the King was challenged, both as head of the Church and of the State. By the end of the seventeenth century, a degree of compromise and stability had been achieved which was the basis of profound agricultural and industrial changes during the following century.

These issues are too complex for young children to tackle in a genuine problem-solving way. However, the focuses chosen do reflect the key issues and aim to translate them into a form which children can grapple with. The focus on houses included a visit to Hampton Court, the show-piece of Henry VIII's new style of government and also to a nearby timber-frame Elizabethan house, representing the increasing wealth and stability of the new 'gentry'. The visit to the Mary Rose reflected the emergence of the ships and sea-power which created their wealth. The Civil War was approached through a large reconstruction of the siege of Newark, based on a contemporary plan, and through discussing how valid the diary of Lucy Hutchinson, wife of the Roundhead commander of Nottingham castle may be. Visits to study portraits of the period, and everyday furniture and artefacts rooted the political events firmly in the context of peoples' everyday experiences at a level at which children can learn to make deductions. (The group who visited the Geffrye Museum borrowed seventeenth-century costumes from the local College of Further Education, which they displayed on models, in a Stuart 'room' constructed in a corner by projecting slides of interiors from the museum on to the surrounding screens then painting them accurately. They wrote a brochure explaining the significance of the furniture and costumes.)

An excellent opportunity for giving the Tudor unit a multicultural dimension was discovered in a Schools Council booklet 'Akbar and Elizabeth' (1983). This shows teachers how they can help children to discover from Indian miniatures (in the Victoria and Albert Museum) the rich cross-cultural influences between India and England in the reign of Elizabeth I through comparing clothes, buildings and garden design.

As part of the focus on ships, both Year 5 and Year 6 spent two weeks finding out about the Armada. The competition between Britain and Spain to find new routes to India and the East Indies, and the ensuing conflict in central America and the West Indies, underlined by religious differences, was explained in class lessons. The viewpoints of different groups were discussed. How would the English Protestants feel, the English Catholics, the French, the Dutch, the Spanish? Why might the Scots be ambivalent? Children then worked in groups or individually to find out all they could about the daily progress of the Armada, making charts, maps and diaries. They made a display of daily rations for a Spanish and an English sailor, pie charts of the estimated food needed on a ship, and graphs showing ships of different kinds. Finally, each class worked in six groups together with the advisory teachers for Information Technology; by the end of a day, each group succeeded in producing a 'broadsheet' giving news of the Armada from the standpoint of a particular group. The French produced 'La Grenouille', the Spanish 'L'Escorial', the English Protestants 'The Golden Hind', the English Catholics 'the Priesthole' and the Scots 'the Record'. Later, they evaluated the extent to which they had reflected different attitudes. These examples show that children are considering the reasons for behaviour and events. (Attainment target 1, strand (b), levels 2–5). This was followed by looking for bias in recent newspapers on a topical issue.

Diagram 4.7: Core study unit 2. Key stage 2– Tudor times (Part one)

History

(i) Time-line 1485–1603

(ii) Tudor houses
(a) Visit to Hampton Court: interpreting evidence – chapel cushions, kitchen, chimneys, astronomical clock, tapestries, drains.
(b) Timber-frame buildings. Use inventory to furnish your house.

(iii) Tudor ships
(a) Visit to Mary Rose. Interpreting evidence, weapons, clothes, leisure.
(b) The Armada.
(iv) Reconstructions.

Maths

(i) Estimate size of a particular house, measure, draw nets to scale, construct, fill in sheet on concepts learned: (measures, ratio, shape and space).

(ii) Voyages of exploration: time and distance calculations.

(iii) Data presentation – Tudor sailors' diet.

Science

(i) Testing roof truss designs. Designing and making a timber frame barn in balsa wood.

(ii) Astronomical clock (earth in space . . .).

(iii) Mass Density Gravity Experiments. } why did the Mary Rose sink?

R.E.

The Reformation.
Different ways of worshipping God – now and then.
Conscience: Thomas More and Elizabethan martyrs.
Politics and religion.

Music

Tallis and Arne.
Listen to tapes.
Play on recorders.
Make up Tudor dances.

Art

(i) Design book covers based on 'Elizabethan Embroidery' Victoria and Albert Museum. HMSO (1968). or on lino-print of political cartoon.

(ii) Drawings at Hampton Court and Mary Rose for class museum.

(iii) Portraits of Henry VIII, of Elizabeth I. What do they tell us? How valid are they as evidence?

Geography

(1) Trade routes to India and East Indies (spices, gold, silver, silk), to West Indies (sugar cane, silver, gold).
Competition and piracy with Spain.
Descriptions of relations with local communities from points of view of indigenous Indians, Spanish, British, and West Africans.

(2) Akbar the Great.
Mughal miniatures: garden, dress, buildings – cultural influences on Elizabethan England.

English

(i) Class novel: 'A Traveller in Time' – A. Uttley.

(ii) Discussion of evidence . . . . .

(iii) Armada Day. Collect information about Armada from different viewpoints (Dutch, French, Spanish, Scots, English Protestants, English RCs). In groups, write broadsheet from your point of view. Write it and produce using IT (front page). Evaluate your group and paper. Compare with newspaper accounts from different viewpoints today.

Diagram 4.8: *Tudor and Stuart times – history grid for the Tudors*

What I want children to learn	What I want children to do	Assessment
AT 1		
3 (a) Describe changes over a period of time	(i) Make a class time-line 1485–1603 Put on key events learned through class lessons and reference work: e.g. Reformation, voyages of exploration, Armada, Monarchs	3 (a) Give a presentation describing changes shown in time-line for an audience.
(b) Give a reason for a historical event or development		3 (b) Explain some of the changes (causes and consequences of Reformation or of Drake's voyages to central America, or reasons for development of large Tudor houses.)
4 (a) Recognise that over time some things changed and some things stayed the same	(ii) In groups make 'way of life' time-lines for buildings, clothes, music, and drama	4 (a) Can make sets of 'things that changed' and 'things that stayed the same'.
(b) Show awareness that historical events usually have more than one cause and consequence	Hang on pictures and information found out about them	4 (b) Devise 'chaining' game which involves (orally or through devising 'clue' cards) thinking of all possible causes of e.g. Reformation or explorers' voyages or Tudor houses.
(c) Describe different features of a historical period		4 (c) Can explain and cross-refer different 'ways of life' time-lines.
5 (c) Show how different features or a historical situation relate to each other		5 (c) Can play a game involving selecting 'cause' or consequence cards for a situation (see 4 b) and can explain what links there are between them.

Diagram 4.8: *Cont. AT2 has been defined as concerned with subsequent reconstructions of a period in the past (see page 68)*

What I want children to learn	What I want children to do	Assessment
AT 2		
2 Show awareness that different stories about the past give different versions of what happened.	(i) Become aware of different ways of representing domestic life in Tudor times by collecting reconstructions (e.g. of 'Living History', English Heritage Education Service; extracts from *A Traveller in Time*, A. Uttley, concerned with food, meals, cooking; extracts from *Black Adder*, BBC TV; nursery rhyme illustrations apparently set in Tudor times: *The Queen of Hearts*).	2 Can describe differences between reconstructions, why they were made, for whom, and which ones are most believable.
3 Distinguish between a fact and a point of view.	(ii) Pretend to be members of a jury, presented with one of the above reconstructions. Discuss what you think is true and what is 'made up'.	3 Can make sets of 'things based on evidence' and 'things which are made up'.
4 Show understanding that deficiencies in evidence may lead to different interpretations.	(iii) Groups make up own plays about preparing a Tudor meal based on evidence in order to investigate differences between versions of the past.	4 Can explain what is 'made up' in their reconstruction (e.g. feelings, relationships).
5 Recognise that interpretations may differ from what is known to have happened.	(iv) Use information books and primary sources to find out more about food available, recipes (English Heritage Publications), furniture, utensils and manners (e.g. *The Elizabethan Age, Books 1 and 2*, P. & M. Speed, Oxford University Press) *Lord Cobham and his family at table* (painting in Blyth, J. 1989).	5 Can write 'advice' for producers of the reconstructions in (i), on how to make their work more authentic, and/or write a reply from producer saying why they do/do not wish to. (This could be done as rôle-play rather than letter-writing).

Diagram 4.8: *Cont*

What I want children to learn	What I want children to do	Assessment
AT 3	1. Visit to Hampton Court (see web). Drawings and photographs, used in school as clues to find out what they may tell us about Henry VIII and his Court.	
2 Recognise that historical sources can help to answer questions		2 Can formulate own questions before the visit.
3 Make deductions from historical sources	2. Visit to Mary Rose and Museum, Portsmouth. Drawings and photographs to interpret as clues to life on a Tudor ship.	3 Can suggest what chosen evidence may tell us about the past.
4 Put together information drawn from different sources	Present in Class Museum or Book or on video or oral tape for audience.	4 Can present variety of evidence, possibly using one piece to answer a question raised by another piece of evidence (e.g. how was the gun fired?).
5 Comment on the usefulness of a source for a particular enquiry		5 Can explain what we do *not* know from this evidence (e.g. who were the people on board, exactly how was the ship built, or why did it sink?).

Diagram 4.9: *Plan showing how work for the term was organised around three focuses*

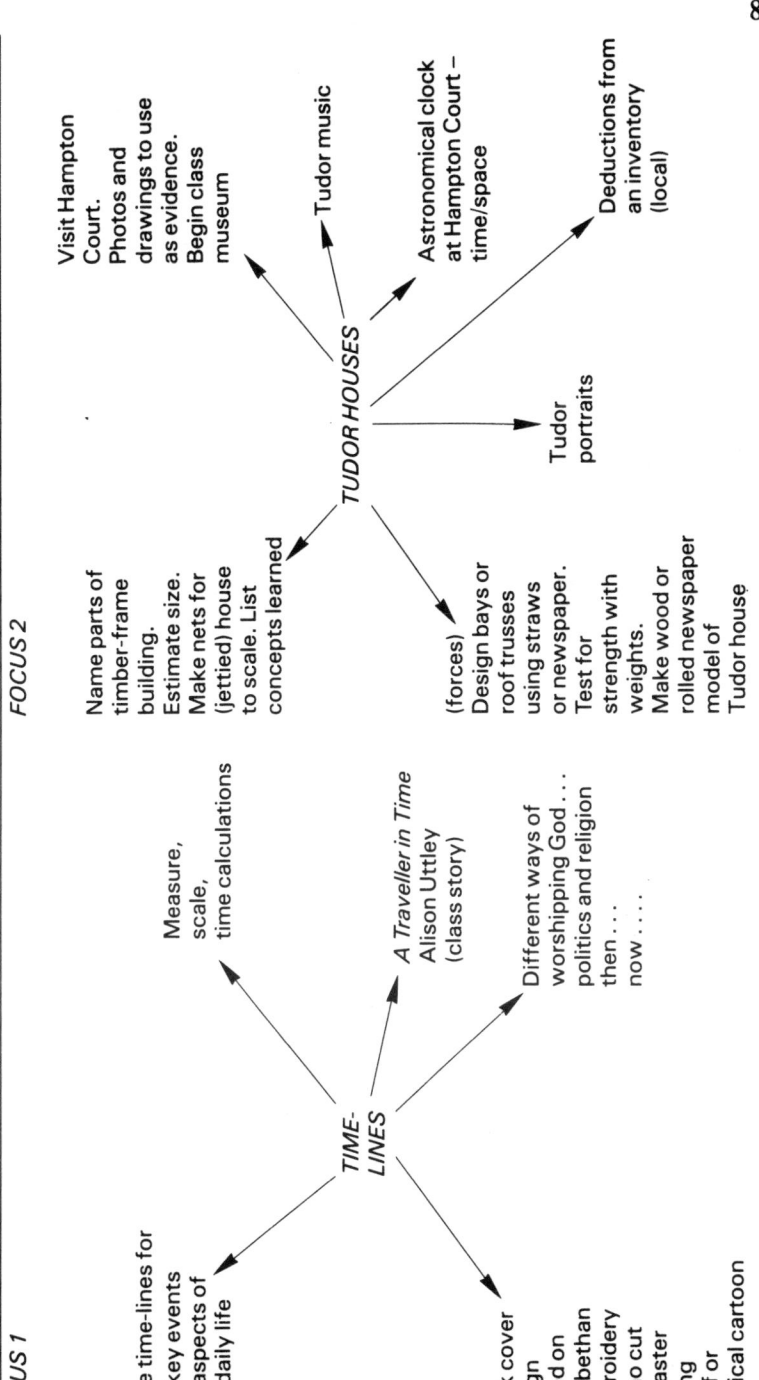

FOCUS 1

FOCUS 2

TUDOR HOUSES

Visit Hampton Court. Photos and drawings to use as evidence. Begin class museum

Tudor music

Astronomical clock at Hampton Court – time/space

Deductions from an inventory (local)

Tudor portraits

Name parts of timber-frame building. Estimate size. Make nets for (jettied) house to scale. List concepts learned

(forces) Design bays or roof trusses using straws or newspaper. Test for strength with weights. Make wood or rolled newspaper model of Tudor house

TIME-LINES

Measure, scale, time calculations

A Traveller in Time Alison Uttley (class story)

Different ways of worshipping God … politics and religion then … now …..

Make time-lines for
(1) key events
(2) aspects of daily life

Book cover design based on Elizabethan embroidery or lino cut of plaster ceiling relief or political cartoon

Diagram 4.9: *Cont*

FOCUS 3

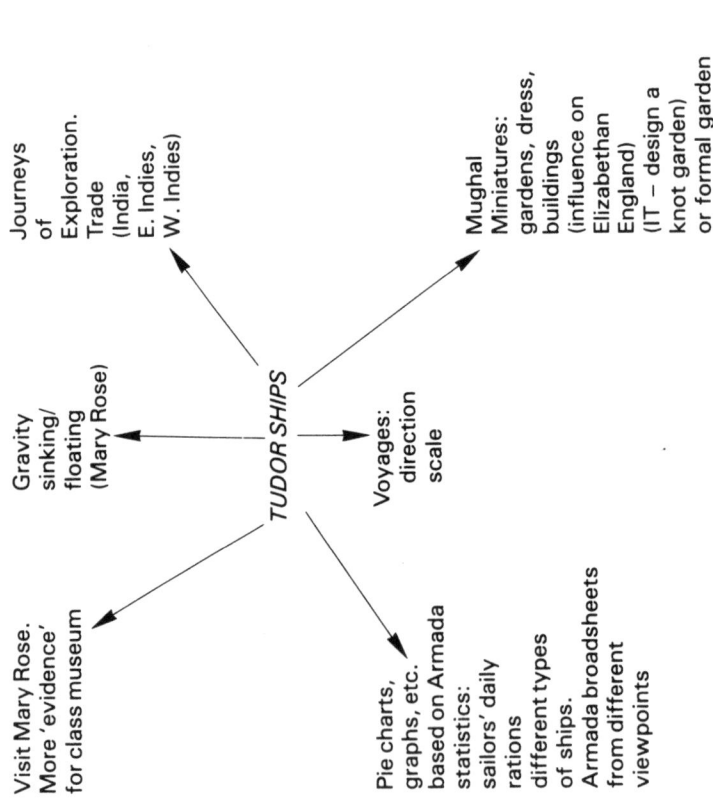

Visit Mary Rose.
More 'evidence'
for class museum

Gravity
sinking/
floating
(Mary Rose)

Journeys
of
Exploration.
Trade
(India,
E. Indies,
W. Indies)

TUDOR SHIPS

Voyages:
direction
scale

Mughal
Miniatures:
gardens, dress,
buildings
(influence on
Elizabethan
England)
(IT – design a
knot garden)
or formal garden

Pie charts,
graphs, etc.
based on Armada
statistics:
sailors' daily
rations
different types
of ships.
Armada broadsheets
from different
viewpoints

The extracts from broadsheets representing different points of view were written on 'Armada Day'. They are based on 'press releases' and information in simulated teletext using 'Simtex', prepared by the Croydon Humanities adviser, Don Garman.

LA GRENOUILLE

6f

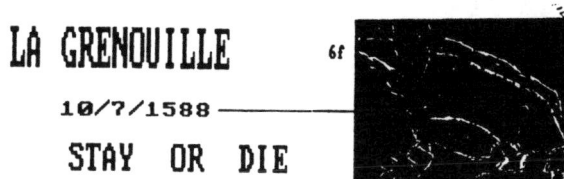

10/7/1588

STAY OR DIE

The Duke of Madina Sidonia commented that if any Spanish Captain fails to maintain his position the penalty would be death, by hanging.
Soon the English are expected to run out of ammunition and surrender to the Spanish and the noble king Phillip II is once more going to demonstrate his enormous power. We are all behind him in the forthcoming final few battles at the sea.

THE PRIESTHOLE

1d

11 AUGUST 1588

SAIL AWAY, SAIL AWAY, SAIL AWAY

9 July 1588 6.0pm Captain Fleming of the Golden Hind has sigalled the sighting of the Spanish fleet off the Lizard.
The tide will not allow the English fleet at Plymouth under Admiral Lord Howard of Effingham to put to sea till 9.0pm.
4 vessels of the English fleet managed to use their boats and anchors to warp out of Plymouth harbour before 9.0pm.
July 30 3.0pm Armada sighted by the English fleet to the south of Eddystone Lighthouse.
Beacons are reported to have been lit from Cornwall to London, local militia being organised to defend the English coastline.
July 31st the English pinnace Disdain opened fire off Plymouth at the rata encoranada.
At 9.0am this morning the Spanish flagship raised her national flag to signal the beginnning.
After a four hour battlethe Armada continues eastwood with the English in pursuit.Medina Sadonya gives the order for the fleet to form a cresant with the more heavily armed ships positioned at the horns.Drake reportedto have left fleet during the night to investigate sails to the south.

L' ESCORIEL

2D

JULY 1588

HE MUCKED UP OUR -
INVASION PLAN

He Duke of Palma mucked up our invasion plan because he was not ready in Dunkruk to sail.

Philip II was very angry when he found out,On the other hand Philip was pleased with The Duke of Medina Sidonia because he had reached Calais not losing too many ships and not having a sea battle with Englande.

After this achievement,How did the Duke of Palma dare to say that his 17,000 men,1000 cavalry,170 ships would not be ready for 2 weeks.

Which side was God on?

THE GOLDEN HIND

1gr

1st August 1588

ARMADA SIGHTED

It was two weeks ago at south of Eddy-stone Lighthouse that the Armada was spotted by the English Fleet.1 week ago the English Fleet positioned themselves behind the Spanish Fleet and had the advantage of being windward.A couple of days ago the prize ship"San Salvardor" arrived at Weymouth badly damaged.We think that there was an explosion below decks. There were quite a few smoke blackened corpses on board.

Fight for Elizabeth.

—She is our Queen—

FIRE SHIPS

A plan to send out some fire ships to Calais harbour in France is still to be decided on for Queen Elizabeth is not sure whether it is a good idea.

THE ORANGE
AUG 1599

THE DUTCH LURE

We have been looking at our reports and they say that England are going to win.We do hope so.when we went to interview Lord Effingham he said thay have a good chance of winning.Spains ships are sinking by the hour and about 1,50 men have been killed. We will continue this story next week.

THE RECORD
4 D
AUGUST 14

THE ARMADA

PHILIP OR ELIZABETH
There has been months of conflict between England and Spain.Does it really matter to us Scots ? Our contacts inform us that defences have been set up in England,because rumours of the invasion,beacons have been set up in selected areas.
Rumours of Philips invasion plan have leeked out of Spain,he plans to make Elizabeth 1 pay for the invasion 2 stop helping the Dutch 3 stop killing catholics.

The seventeenth-century unit began with an outline of the causes and events of the Civil War. The Year 5 class were spending one afternoon every fortnight with the local high school on a technology liaison project. They based their technology work on the plan given in Paul Noble's book (1986) of the Siege of Newark. They converted the scale to metric measurements (this involved considerable calculations), then made a scale model, complete with cannons, ammunition stores, fences, stables and wooden living quarters.

More mathematics was related to making nets for models of particular timber-frame houses: estimation, ratio, measurement, properties of cuboids and prisms; making a sequence of cuboid jetties

Diagram 4.10: *Core study unit 2. Key stage 2 Stuart times – (Part two)*

Maths

1. Large-scale map of Siege of Newark, measures, calculations (furlongs and metres).
2. Multiplication (Pepys' Diary). What calculations might Pepys have to make in supplying navy?
3. Investigations – Halley's Comet.
4. Devices for measuring solar time – pendulum clocks (Maritime Museum).
5. Plague statistics.

English

1. Speaking and listening: note-taking, discussing evidence, role-play; story of the witches of Pendle.
2. Reading; reference work.
3. Writing: picture stories, interpreting evidence, mathematics explanations, science experiments.

Science/Technology

1. Newton – gravity.
2. Lenses, prisms, light.
3. The earth in space (Maritime Museum).
4. Harvey. Circulation of the blood. (Pulse experiments, breathing . . .).
5. Technology – make model of Siege of Newark.

Art

1. Draw artefacts seen in museums.
2. Bent light rays – colour, lenses to enlarge design.
3. Pottery models – Roundheads and Cavaliers for Siege model.
4. Needlework based on Dutch tulip design or Jacobean design.
5. Bookmaking.

History

1. Civil War. Siege of Nottingham. Lucy Hutchinson's diary.
2. Fire of London. Pepys' Diary. Wren's designs for London after the Fire.
3. Superstition and belief.
4. Visit. Either Portrait Gallery or Geffrye Gallery or Museum of London (choice).
5. Interpretations: Subsequent descriptions of Charles I.

Geography

1. British Isles. Civil War. Key places then (now?) (why?).
2. Wren's design for rebuilding London. Compare with map today. Was it adopted? Why not? Should it have been? Identify place names and seventeenth-century buildings.

Music

Traditional seventeenth-century folk tunes (e.g. Here's a Health Unto His Majesty, Lillibullero).

Seventeenth-century hymn tunes.

R.E.

The English Prayer book.

Different Christian Church buildings – why?

Prayers and churches in other cultures – different ways of expressing and celebrating beliefs.

Diagram 4.11: *Stuart times – history grid for the Stuarts*

What I want children to learn	What I want children to do	Assessment
AT 1		
3 (a) Describe changes over a period of time	Make class time-line 1603–1714	3 (a) Can describe information shown on time-line
(b) Give a reason for a historical event or development	Find out about and put on it: key people (monarchs), key events (gunpowder plot, Civil War, Restoration). (If possible, find out about local families during Civil War)	(b) Can give a reason for a key event (or explain allegiances of a local family)
4 (a) Recognise that some things changed and some things stayed the same		4 (a) Can make sets of things which changed and things which did not
(b) Show awareness that events usually have more than one cause and consequence	Make group time-lines for buildings, music and drama, scientific discoveries, costume . . . . Collect information, illustrate and place on time-lines	(b) Role-play parliamentary debate stating reasons why/not Charles I should be opposed
(c) Describe different features of a historical period		(c) Collate, as pamphlet, information from variety of time-lines
5 (a) Distinguish between different kinds of historical change		5 (a) (b) and can explain why changes on different time-lines occurred
(b) Identify different types of cause and consequence		
(c) Show how different features in a historical situation relate to each other		(c) Can connect changes on different time-lines

Diagram 4.11: *Cont. AT2 has been defined as concerned with subsequent reconstructions of a period in the past (see page 68)*

What I want children to learn	What I want children to do	Assessment
AT2		
2 Show awareness that different stories about the past can give different versions of what happened.	(i) Become aware of different ways of representing the past by collecting images and descriptions made in subsequent times, of Charles I (e.g. cut-out cardboard figure, replica Royalist badge and coin set, History in Evidence, Chesterfield S42 5UY; description of Cavaliers in *1066 and All That*, Sellars, W.C. and Yeatman, R.J. p. 71 (1973).	2 Can exhibit and label one of these reconstructions, saying who made it, why, and when.
3 Distinguish between a fact and a point of view.	(ii) Tape-record brief description of Charles I from children's book, pausing at end of each phrase. Put tape-recording in above exhibition. Construct electric button 'buzzer'. Visitors to exhibition press buzzer every time they hear a 'fact'.	3 Can recognize 'facts' in recorded description of Charles I and press 'buzzer' appropriately. Can fill in 'visitor's questionnaire' saying how many 'facts' they think there were.
4 Show understanding that differences in evidence may lead to different interpretations.	(iii) In pairs record 'in-depth interviews', one child 'in role' as Charles I, the other asking questions based on what they know of an event in the life of Charles I.	4 Can comment on why the interviews produce different accounts.
5 Recognise that interpretations of the past may differ from what is known to have happened.	(iv) Make up a 'Black Adder-style' entertainment programme based on an event in the seventeenth century. (This could be compared with a reconstruction by the Sealed Knot (Paul Cunningham, Fern Cottage, Torn Barton, Norton St. Philip, BA36 6LN.)).	5 Can write a critical letter of protest from a 'serious historian', and/or can write a letter of reply from the producer explaining why the programme was made.

Diagram 4.11: *Cont*

What I want children to learn	What I want children to do	Assessment
AT 3		
2 Recognise historical sources can answer questions	Write questions about a portrait (postcard) as a quiz for others (e.g. after visiting Portrait Gallery)	2 Can write quiz about portrait.
3 Make deductions from sources		3 Can answer someone else's portrait quiz or can write account of Fire of London based on information in Pepys' Diary.
4 Put together information from different sources	Draw artefacts or collect pictures in Geffrye Museum or Museum of London	4 Can make a class display with accompanying brochure.
5 Comment on the usefulness of a source for a particular enquiry	Visit Museum with a question to investigate (e.g. what happened if you were ill in the seventeenth century or if your home caught fire or how you might light your house.	5 Write to the Museum saying in what way you found their collection helpful in your work 'as a historian'.

Diagram 4.12: *Plan showing how work for the term was organised around four focuses*

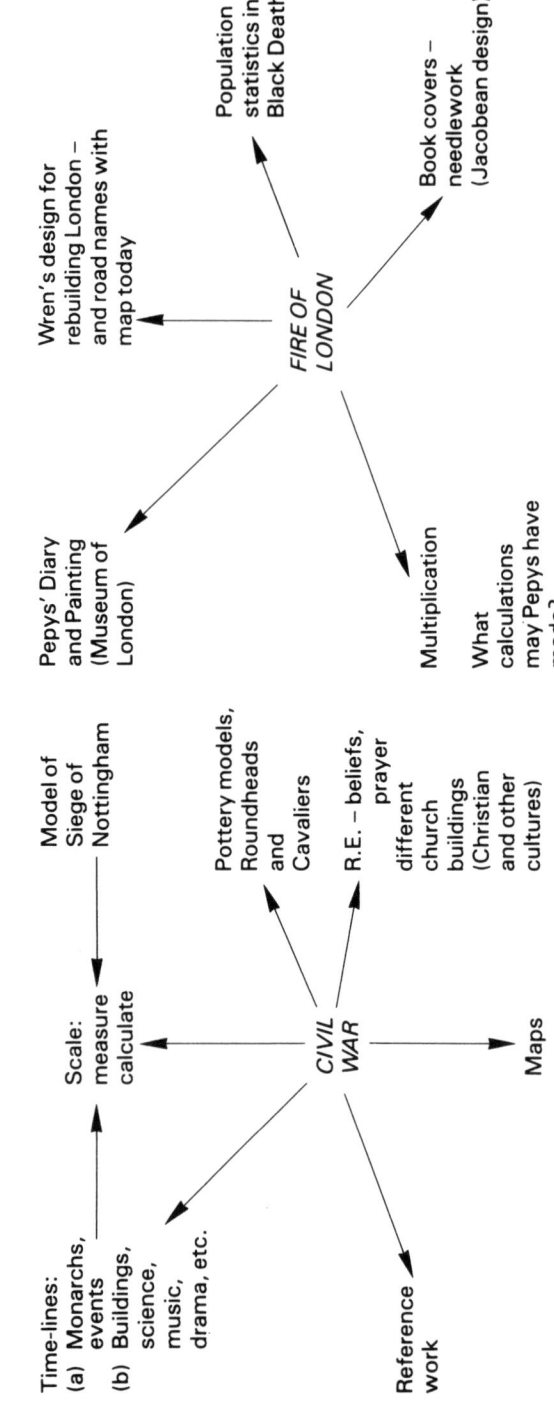

FOCUS 1

FOCUS 2

Time-lines:
(a) Monarchs,
    events
(b) Buildings,
    science,
    music,
    drama, etc.

Scale:
measure
calculate

Model of
Siege of
Nottingham

Pepys' Diary
and Painting
(Museum of
London)

Wren's design for
rebuilding London –
and road names with
map today

Population
statistics in
Black Death

Pottery models,
Roundheads
and
Cavaliers

R.E. – beliefs,
prayer
different
church
buildings
(Christian
and other
cultures)

CIVIL
WAR

Maps

Reference
work

FIRE OF
LONDON

Multiplication

What
calculations
may Pepys have
made?

Book covers –
needlework
(Jacobean design)

Diagram 4.12: *Cont*

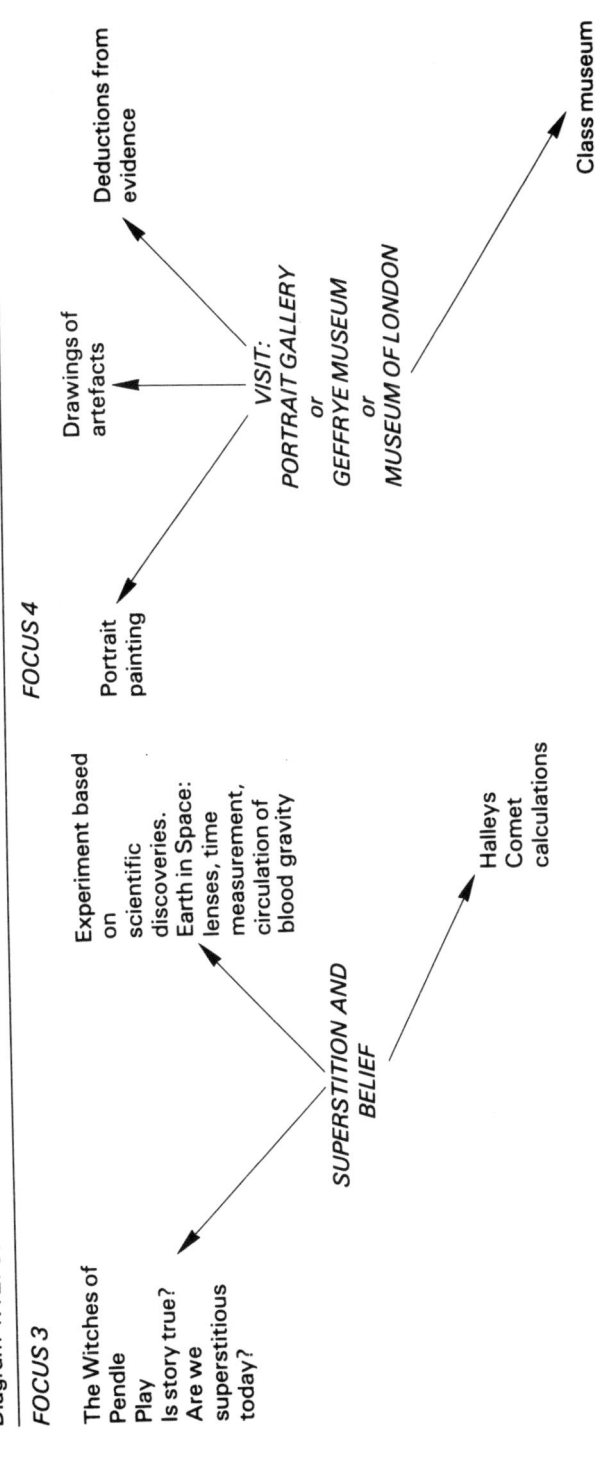

FOCUS 3

The Witches of
Pendle
Play
Is story true?
Are we
superstitious
today?

*SUPERSTITION AND
BELIEF*

Experiment based
on
scientific
discoveries.
Earth in Space:
lenses, time
measurement,
circulation of
blood gravity

Halleys
Comet
calculations

FOCUS 4

Portrait
painting

Drawings of
artefacts

Deductions from
evidence

*VISIT:
PORTRAIT GALLERY
or
GEFFRYE MUSEUM
or
MUSEUM OF LONDON*

Class museum

needed some thought. The discovery that Pepys took lessons in multiplication in his late twenties, in order to do the calculations necessary for supplying the British Navy, and his decision that his wife should also learn her tables, led to interesting work on multiplication, across a range of levels. Children had to decide on a calculation Pepys may have needed to make, how many barrels of beef may be needed for one ship, or how many fir trees for masts for 'x' many ships, then they had to find as many ways as possible of finding the answer. This involved a certain amount of historical research to find out how many men there may be on a ship, and how long it may be at sea. The importance of using and applying mathematics in a context was illustrated by one boy with a number of learning difficulties. His calculation was correct, but written in very wobbly writing. 'Is anything the matter M?' the teacher asked. 'But Miss,' he protested, 'I was on shipboard!' More calculations were precipitated by the discovery that Halley predicted an orbit of 76 years for the comet named after him in 1677, including the sad conclusion that the teacher would never see it!

Questions on King Charles I

Q 1. What tells you that he is a King?

Q 2. What does the blue sash mean.?

Q 3 Why is there a pillar behind King Charles.?

Q 4. Why is his hair longer on Charles left.?

Q5 What material is the curtian behind him?

Q6 How many different kinds of stones are in the Crown.?

Q 7 Why has he got a stick in his hand.?

The children who visited the Portrait Gallery had painted portraits of each other first, and discussed how much it is possible to tell about a person from a portrait, and why. After the visit, they each wrote a quiz, about a postcard of one of the portraits they had studied.

A 1. The crown jewels, the sword, his Clothes, velvet curtains, and his spurs.

A 2. The blue sash means that he is a Knight of the garter

A 3. The Pillar makes him look big and important.

A 4. That was the fasson for rich people in those days.

A 5. The material is felt.

A 6. Five: Saphires, Rube's, Emeralds, Diamonds, and (peals) peral's.

A 7. He has a stick to make him look important.

This attempt to assess the accuracy of Lucy Hutchinson's account of the Siege of Nottingham shows that the child is trying to reason in his own way, and to apply the information he has, (even though he changed his opinion dramatically, convinced by his own sexist argument!)

Children might also be interested in extracts from the diaries of Lady Anne Clifford (1590–1676), published by Alan Sutton Ltd 1990. They record how this determined seventeenth-century woman fought her husband, her uncle and the King for the right to inherit her lands in

11.188

A Dispute on Lucy Hutchinson's Account of the Royalist Attack on Nottingham

I believe that it may be partly true. Because she was there and also her husband, Colonel John Hutchinson, was the Commander of Nottingham Castle. (Was) It was also possible because the Cavaliers carried muskets and cavalrymen carry swords so that may have been why the Roundheads retreated.

It is more likely though to have been a pack of unintentional lies! She wouldn't of (har) dared to go to the window incase she got shot and she wouldn't of gone out without protection with a metre stick into Cavalier (territory) territory, measuring all the way! From the window she

wouldn't be able to see the blood
through the trees, even without leaves
on them. If her husband cared-about
her she wouldn't of gone out until
the bodies were cleared. So I say
it is not true at all.

Deductions from the plan of the Siege of Newark involved complicated calculations!

The width of the town of Newark is

6 Furlongs

$\frac{3}{4}$ miles

1200 metres

The length of beacon hill is 8 Furlongs

1 mile

1600 metres

The width of beacon hill is 4 Furlongs

$\frac{1}{2}$ mile

800 metres

The length of the river trent is 80 Furlong

10 miles

160,00 metres

General Henrys troops would have
to march 18 Furlongs to reach the town of
Newark. 24 miles

3600 metres

the north of England. She finally did so at the age of 53, and managed them effectively for the next 33 years. The diaries begin with 15-year-old Anne Clifford watching the funeral procession of Queen Elizabeth. They tell us about her life in the country and at court, and also about her favourite clothes, her infant daughter and, later, grandchildren and the members of her household.

Models of timber-frame houses, based on particular examples, involved a range of mathematical concepts: measure, scale, properties of solid shapes. This is part of a child's self-evaluation sheet, made when he had finished his model, to explain the mathematics he thought he had learned in making it.

Mathematics
I learned Making
Tudor House Models.

length estimate measure	metres centimetre	I estimated the height of my house as 4m.
Scale	1:100	The lenght of my house in real life would be 12m and on my model it is 12cm
Convert from one unit to another.	metres to cm cm to mm (to nearest mm)	The width of my house is 6m which on my model would be 6cm it could also be 6mm. 6m = 600cm = 6000mm
area rectangle triangle	cm^2 m^2	the area of my first rectangle is 72cm^2. The area of my roof is 16cm^2
Volume of cuboid	cm^3 m^3	The volume of my 2nd cuboid is 252cm^3.

Properties	faces	On a cuboid there
of solid shapes	edges	is 6 faces
Cuboid	angles	12 edges 24 angles
△ based prism	faces edges angles	5 faces 9 edges 12 angles
measuring angles right angle		the right angle on my roof is 90°. the right angle on the side of my roof is 90°
acute angle		there are 4 acute angle on my house. the acute angles are 45°
obtuse angle		there are 0 obtuse angles on my house.

CHAPTER 5

Professional Development

In this chapter three workshops will be described, which aimed to develop teachers' confidence in teaching history in the primary school, by themselves experiencing the processes involved in learning about the past through active problem-solving, at their own level. They could then translate these processes into experiences suitable for children of different ages. The workshops were of different durations; a residential weekend, a day and a half-day session. There is a slowly increasing number of opportunities for in-service education in primary history teaching organised by Local Education Authorities, and by the Department of Education and Science, as well as excellent sessions run by English Heritage, by galleries and museums. The examples given are simply ideas, based on experience, for workshops which groups of teachers could undertake for themselves. Teachers who took part found them useful, they produced subsequent good work from children, and, above all, the sessions were remembered as enjoyable. 'If only all INSET was such good fun' one teacher said at a chance meeting several years later. 'Good fun' is an essential ingredient of all education, including that of teachers!

A residential weekend

This took place at the Commonwork Centre, Bore Place, Chiddingstone, Kent. It is a farm whose documented history goes back to the thirteenth century, which is run both as a dairy farm and a study centre. Archaeologists and historians are working with ecologists, geographers and agriculturalists, in an integrated interdisciplinary study to provide both a record of the past and a guide for future conservation and development. They have collected numerous documents, legal, agricultural and personal. There is visible evidence

106

of successive changes in the buildings; a Tudor manor house, incorporated into a Jacobean mansion with recent additions, seventeenth-century barns, and an eighteenth-century oast house. Woods, hedges, ponds and streams reveal the management practices of generations of farmers.

The aim of the weekend was to try to find out what Bore Place was like in the seventeenth century. In doing so, it was hoped that teachers would experience the processes of historical enquiry, and also other aspects of good primary practice themselves. They could work at their own level, independently and in collaborative groups, experience the problems and satisfaction of using a variety of sources, learn through activities, see the interrelationship of disciplines, record their findings in a variety of ways, and, finally, present them to an audience. The objectives were set out as:

(1) To consider how the landscape can be used to develop an understanding of the following humanities concepts:
    (a) Evidence
    (b) Change and continuity
    (c) Causation
    (d) Empathy.
(2) To consider and experience how the landscape can be used as a resource for language development.
(3) To consider, develop and practice skills related to enquiry in the humanities.
(4) To consider and practice ways of recording observations and conclusions, e.g. writing, drama, data-bases, computer graphics, art and craft work.
(5) To consider how the Bore Place experience can be replicated in our own teaching contexts.

The programme was:

Diagram 5.1: *Programme for the weekend at Bore Place*

Time	Activities	Teachers' Responses
Friday		
5–6 pm	Tea and unpack	
6–7 pm	Dinner (plenty of wine)	
7–7.30 pm	Meet in the old barn. Groups given time-line 1600–1700, and list of events related to politics, science, literature, agriculture, music, (e.g. accession of monarchs,	(a) Quick telephone calls by organisers who had lost list of correct answers and did not know most of them (concealed in order not to diminish confidence in them at this stage!).

Time	Activities	Teachers' Responses

Gunpowder plot, Voyage of Mayflower, Civil War started, Great Fire of London, Sir Isaac Newton's work on gravity published, first Astronomer Royal appointed, Jethro Tull invented seed drill, Paradise Lost, Pilgrims Progress published). Limited time to locate them on time-line.

The aim of this exercise was to get people talking, confident in their shared ignorance of precise dates, seeing that precise dates are not always crucial but that sequences and likely estimates can often be deduced, and also to focus people's minds on an overview of the century in question, drawing on whatever existing knowledge they could bring to bear on it.

(b) Teachers amazed at their shared amounts of knowledge, and already engaged in animated argument, using vocabulary such as caused, because, what if, why not, therefore, earlier, later . . . .

7.30–9.00 pm

Whole group activity: making deductions from evidence. The aim was to introduce the idea that evidence can be used to find out about the past, that different sources offer different kinds of information, and that interpretations must be valid (i.e. not contradicted by other evidence, in line with what is known of the period, logical). Interpretations must recognise bias and incompleteness. Therefore, the importance of a discursive approach was stressed.

(i) Quotation from
1066 and all That
Charles was a Cavalier King and therefore had a small pointed beard, long flowing

Time	Activities	Teachers' Responses

curls, a large, flat, flowing hat and *gay attire*. The Roundheads, on the other hand were clean-shaven and wore tall conical hats, white ties and *sombre* garments. Under those circumstances, a Civil War was inevitable. (Sellars and Yeatman, 1973, p.71)
This was contrasted with an active problem-solving approach to teaching history.

(ii) Evidence: furniture, portraits, diaries
(a) Slides, Geffrye Museum: Stuart Room 1668. William and Mary Room 1690.
Stuart Room 1668

1. Fireback	Iron. From the Weald? . . .
Thick wine bottle	Disposable bottles? . . .
Settle, panelling	Oak and leather . . . Not very comfortable . . . Long lasting . . . handed on . . . Functional, solid.
Bed-hanging	Bedrooms interconnecting ∴ Bed-hangings to ensure privacy . . . (various other comments . . .)
Candelabra	Long, dark nights . . . beeswax. What did the poor have?
Chair	Cane from China, French walnut – French influence (trade and contact with a wider world). Tall back ∴ Later furniture shows status.
Portraits – family, children	Continuity is important.

William and Mary Room 1690

Painting – seascape	Dutch Realistic Attitude to/pleasure in environment
Chinese bowl	Trade – emerging new class with wealth based on trade. Trade with China

Time	Activities	Teachers' Responses
	Harpsichord	Domestic music-making What music?
	(b) Slides – portraits *Charles I* 1631. Daniel Mytens	
	How do you know he is a king? Why is he standing in front of a pillar? What else tells you he is powerful? What do you think this portrait tells us about Charles I?	Crown, orb, sceptre Strength, height, power Sword, spurs, clothes, Order of the Garter Fashionable hairstyle Image he wanted to convey?
	Oliver Cromwell 1649. Robert Walker	
	Why is he carrying a baton under his arm? What does his dress tell you? What does the background suggest? What do you think he was like?	Armour – strength, fighting Sash – Roundhead Puritan collar – attitudes
	Diary of Samuel Pepys (1987) The Plague (pp. 494, 496, 498, 500, 506, 519)	How Plague strikes, protection against it, how dead buried, numbers dead.
	Both the Friday evening activities aimed to introduce broad national background to which the specific local evidence investigated the following day could be related.	
Saturday 9–10 am	'Perceptive walk' to consider location of farm from different vantage points in relation to landscape, and also to respond to environment through senses.	Smell herbs; listen to sounds (draw 'sound picture'); climb the 'mound' (what is it: earthwork, fortification, folly?). Observe rabbits in warren; hand-made bricks from local clay, different bonds; feel heavy clay soil.

Time	Activities	Teachers' Responses
10.30 am–5.30 pm	Form groups for enquiry sessions described below: The land The people The buildings	
8.30 pm	Saturday evening allowed a visit to the Castle Inn at Chiddingstone and a late-night inspection of the tomb of Bernard Hyde in the churchyard – a previous owner of Bore Place who, legend has it, lost the family fortune and was buried in curious circumstances.	Speculation on veracity of documented account of funeral when coffin alleged by bearers to have become suddenly weightless while carried to church . . . !
Sunday 9.30–12 noon	*Group enquiry sessions* (cont.) *1. The land* (a) Maps OS, 1838, 1761, Elizabethan. Relate these to what can be seen today. Trace changes: what is same/different: ponds tracks field shapes/sizes field names	Stream on three sides completed by a ditch. Had it been fortified? Old tracks remain. Irregular field shapes and sizes indicate a long process of clearing woodland to provide pasture and arable land. Woods, copses, shaws left as boundaries and to provide timber ∴ timber framed buildings: forge, oasthouse, smithy, barns. Warrens – food, fur (for sale?) Fishponds Orchard – grew? Self-supporting . . . Kitchen meadow
	(b) Identify trees and shrubs Relate maps to hedge-dating Each specie of tree in a 30 m stretch represents 100 years.	Some hedges disappeared – why?

Time	Activities	Teachers' Responses
	(c) Whole group activities: Interview farm manager and elderly hedger who works on estate about changes. Milk cow by hand and by machine. Observe artificial insemination. Discuss breeding and genetics; relate milking and reproduction to spread-sheets of milk yields throughout year. Use old farm implements and move loads by hand. Compare with modern machinery (speed, time, distance experiments).	Hand milking aroused much excitement! Later on one school worked on this aspect to fulfil science AT on genetics. In another school the experiments moving loads were used to introduce a theme which combined 'land transport' with 'forces and energy'.
	2. The people (a) Construct family tree for Hyde family from secondary sources and wills (given examples of letter formation in the seventeenth century in parish registers collected by Society of Genealogists).	Relate this family to national events and trends e.g. Parliamentarian in Civil War, then knighted by Charles II. Changing sources of income. 1603–1631 BH Merchant 1631–1655 BH Merchant and Parliamentarian 1655–1677 John H. Parliamentarian 1677–1685 Sir BH Knighted by Charles II 1685–1719 Humphrey H lawyer 1729–1740 JH lawyer, trade and property in West Indies – loss of fortune

Time	Activities	Teachers' Responses

(b) Inventory.
What do names of room and possessions tell us (e.g. bake house, dairy house, buttery, mill house, brew house, wash house, chandlers house, spinning chamber, parlour, study); 'fishes in all the ponds', 'all the games and conies', 'the mills'. Can rooms be identified today?

Very frustrating. Impossible to identify rooms as part of house removed to a location several miles away in the eighteenth century, and also considerable new additions.

(c) Food.
From inventory and old recipes, construct a seventeenth-century meal using food available on farm at the time. Prepare this for Sunday lunch!
(d) From evidence known about Hyde family, write 'character cards' giving each person's name, and what is known about them from which role-play can be constructed for Sunday lunch. Research other background information (clothes, manners, furniture and cutlery, seating, etc.).

3. The buildings
(a) Relating a seventeenth-century engraving to Bore Place today.

Not realistic representation. Aim was to show status of owner . . . . Limited value . . . .

(b) Farm buildings:
  Oast
  Smithy
  Barns

Research into how beer made, corn threshed and stored.

(c) House
  (i) Timber frame – 3 bays with eighteenth-century facade (finally identified by climbing into roof and tracing roof trusses!)

Very frustrating. Impossible to reconstruct because old bricks and timbers re-used – firebacks may have come from elsewhere, etc.

Time	Activities	Teachers' Responses
	(ii) Bricks – English and Flemish bonds. Handmade.	
	(iii) Panelling – some cut with hand tools and original; some machine-made copies.	
	(iv) Fireplaces – firebacks – very exciting to scratch away soot and reveal Hyde family crest! Also to identify BH incised in beam over fireplace – was this *the* Bernard who lost the family fortune?	
Sunday 1–2.30 pm	*Lunch* Everyone dressed in hired seventeenth-century costume.	No misconceptions that seventeenth-century family did look, feel, or behave much as we did, but 'good fun'!
	Attempt at role-play in characters of Hyde family, with possible events to which they reacted during meal interspersed by 'people' group (e.g. serving wench makes eyes at Parish priest . . .).	Great hilarity . . .
	Lunch consisted of: savoury herb pudding boiled in cloth	Potatoes now replace savoury puddings. Meat broth boiled with it was main meal for poor when cattle and sheep expensive.
	roast, stuffed ox heart	
	ramekin batter	Cooked in 'Dutch' oven – box facing fire with concave interior open to heat.
	sharp egg sauce for chickens (or fish)	Birds in the past were tough!
	mumbled rabbit (minced)	Could be eaten by the toothless! Rabbit was shot on farm – I had the shot!

Time	Activities	Teachers' Responses
	sippet pudding apricot preserve	Importance of preserving food.
	gingerbread potted cheese carrot pudding	Traditional festive treat. Vegetables used in suet puddings (as in Christmas pudding today). Sweet and savoury served together in seventeenth century.
Sunday 2.30–4.00 pm	*Reporting back* for other groups and invited audience, displaying different investigating and recording activities e.g. *The land*: (i) collections of identified and classified trees, shrubs and hedgerow plants, made while hedge-dating. (ii) Collage of Bore Place then and now. *The people*: role-play – reconstructed legal case of dispute over land owner-ship. *The buildings*: timber frame model of old smithy. Handmade bricks made from local clay and fired. Presentation of documentary research related to buildings; difficulties involved.	Much food for thought about how to apply some of the ideas of the weekend to topics for children of different ages and in relation to other places and other periods.

A half day workshop

The aim of this workshop was to consider the nature of historical evidence, then to offer the group (of PGCE students) the opportunity to make appropriate deductions from a range of sources and also to introduce them to the Statements of Attainment for ATs 3 and 2 at either KS 1 or KS 2.

In order to focus student's thinking on the past before the workshop, to involve them in problem-solving which was rooted in their own experiences and interests but did not involve too much preparation, and also to encourage them to get to know something of each other, they had been asked to 'bring in something as old as you, or older'. Before they arrived, a table was covered with attractive drapes and a small but visibly stimulating collection of the tutor's personal artefacts was set out, to which people responded and added their own contributions as they arrived. This was a marvellous ice-breaker, as family photos and heirlooms, things dug up in gardens, or found in junk shops were explained, demonstrated and speculated about.

Introduction - a 'true' story

There are a number of frequently used ways of introducing the concept of historical evidence. The dustbin clues (what we deduce from its contents...?), burying a box (what shall we put in it?) or 'finding a suitcase in the attic' work well. This session began with the broken number plate found outside my house, and the 'true story' of how my husband, suffering from 'flu and with a high temperature the evening before, had heard sounds of an accident outside. Going to the front door, he saw someone leave a white van on the pavement and stagger slowly and unsurely off into the windy, rainy night. He informed the police who took notes, but found no sign of an accident. The next morning, he found the broken number plate, but the van had gone...suspense! What do you think happened? An interesting discussion followed which could be classified under attainment targets 2 and 3, levels 1–4!

Attainment target 2	*Attainment target 3*
(1) Was the person who disappeared into the night a figment of a fevered imagination?	(1) The broken and incomplete number plate was found. It tells us the age of the car, the area where it was bought.
(2) Which is likely to be true, the policeman's report of the facts, or the eyewitness account? Possible versions of who the person was, and what he was doing.	(2) It could tell us who owned the car; they could be traced and asked questions.
(3) Difference between police records and interpretations of account.	(3) We could suggest what sort of a person he was; what he was doing, whether he was driving carefully.

(4) Was the man drunk, hurt, did he skid on wet leaves, avoid a dog or a person, or hit a tree?

(4) A number of accounts could be compared: the driver's account, the eye witness', the policeman's, (the 'defence' and 'prosecution').

The discussion involves certainty and probability and accepting that there are some things which may never be known. It asks questions about how things were made, when, where. It involves oral and written evidence, supporting and contradictory evidence, the status of evidence, a range of interpretations of different levels of likelihood, cause and effect, and the relationship between evidence and the thoughts, feelings and behaviour of people.

Some students later introduced work in history with children by an evidence exercise. John Fusco, introducing work on transport, asked Year 5 children to put things into an imaginary box which could tell a museum owner in a hundred year's time about how we travel in 1991. He found that at first they chose only visual evidence related to their own experience, (a seat belt 'to show we cared about safety', roller skates, model cars and magazine advertisements). When he asked them what sort of a picture this would give, they found it difficult to realise that the museum owner would not have the same knowledge as we have today, but gradually came to see that their collection was selective. They then added photographs of a Rolls Royce and of Concorde, explaining that 'this is how rich people travel', and a life-jacket and an anchor to reflect travel by sea, although they had no experience of this. They also began to propose some written records – a Highway Code and a road map, newspaper articles on a new model of car, and an account of a family cycling around the world. At first the children thought that the deductions which could be drawn in a hundred year's time were factual and descriptive, the colour and shape of cars, or how many people can get on a train, but with prompting they began to consider the attitudes and values, thoughts and feelings which might lie behind the artefacts; would people understand that Reebok trainers are very expensive, and a status symbol amongst children?

Key stage 1, group 1, oral history

This group was given a tape-recording of an elderly lady's memories, supported by an album of photographs of her throughout her life.

Students chose to listen to one of three sections: either 'childhood', or 'high school, university and early teaching career in the 1920s', or 'the evacuation of children during World War II'. They were told to listen to the tape either from the point of view of children (what questions might they ask, and how might they follow up such a session?), or at their own level. It was interesting that different groups, responding at their own level, focused on different aspects but all were incredulous that married women were not allowed to continue to teach (they found it hard to suggest any possible reason), that college students had to wear berets and be indoors at nine o'clock, and that when a young teacher from a poor family, struggling with a reception class of 50 in her first term, caught pneumonia and died in her lodgings, her head-mistress's response was, 'The girl deserved it. She didn't wear woollen combinations.' They were also amazed that this lady had met her former pupils, now all old-age pensioners, at a reunion, the first for over fifty years. One of them had apologised, in tears, for her bad behaviour in class, but explained that she had been abused by her father – an insight her young teacher certainly didn't have in 1932.

Anne-Marie Devereux-Cooke, a KS1 student, decided later to use an oral history approach with Year 1 children. They listened to two accounts of life during the Second World War. The first was a tape-recording of life in a small town in Scotland, and the second was a talk given by a lady who had been a nurse during the London Blitz. The student was particularly interested in some small children's anxiety at being questioned about the accounts individually afterwards, whereas in a group they were able to share their ideas and develop them more confidently. She discussed with the children words particular to the period which had been used (roof-watchers, siren, netting, cables, search lights, home guard), and was surprised by the ability of some children, when the words were focused on, both to work out and explain their meaning, and also to correct misunderstandings revealed by other children.

Cables

Joanne	'They were for when the balloons blew up into the sky . . . and the cables hung down from the balloon, like that.'
Teacher	'And what were they for?'
Amiar	'To kill them.'
Danielle	'No, to make sure the aeroplanes don't come too close. . . .'

Joanne	'The home guard was for watching the . . . .'
James	'The aeroplanes.'
	'To protect you . . . to protect houses . . . .'

In responding to the photographs which one of the ladies, Mrs Isaacs, brought to support her talk (pictures of her wedding, and of her son, born at the end of the war), these five-year-olds spontaneously used time vocabulary.

Joanne	'That was when you were young.'
James	'Not old like you are now.'
Amiar	'Is he a man now?'
Danielle	'Yes, it was a long time ago.'

The children frequently interjected with questions, to gain more information, to clarify and to determine validity. When Mrs Isaacs told them about an incident when her husband had been driving an ambulance in France which went over a landmine and was tossed in the air, James asked:

	'Did the other people in the van were they killed?'
Mrs Isaacs	'Quite a number. I don't know exactly how many. I wasn't there.'
James	'But how do you know if you weren't there? Did he tell you?'
Mrs Isaacs	'I didn't know until I received a letter from him.'
James	'He wrote a letter back, telling you he weren't dead?'
Mrs Isaacs	'That's right.'

Later, the children compiled a questionnaire for Mrs Isaacs of questions which were prompted by her talk. They responded much more actively to this talk than they did to the tape-recording because they were able to interact. However, the children did wonder why the two accounts were so different.

| Joanne | 'They both lived in World War II. Why didn't she (Mrs Wilcockson) say all about the war like Mrs Isaacs did?' |
| James | 'Because they both lived in different countries.' |

They concluded that 'we don't have ration books now', or 'tin hats to protect ourselves, or wear gas masks'.

Key stage 1, group 2, artefacts

This group was asked to make an attractive 'museum display' of the artefacts and photographs contributed, then to list questions they would like to know about them (e.g. what they were, how they worked, who used them, why), and to try to answer them by asking their owners, or by using secondary sources in the library. They could then write a quiz about the exhibits for other students, write explanatory labels or a brochure to accompany the exhibition, or prepare an oral presentation for the end of the session. They were also asked to attempt to sequence the artefacts. Several students subsequently investigated children's ability to make deductions about artefacts, and to sequence artefacts and photographs. Susan Mead investigated the ability of four-year-olds to differentiate between an old and a new doll, and an old and a new teddy, after listening to a story about an old teddy. They concluded that one doll was new because 'she is hard plastic', while the old doll had a china head and a soft body 'full of fluff'. The teddy in the story says that 'you have to come from somewhere to have relatives' and Adam said, 'Everyone has a life-story. It means when you're a baby it starts.'

The teacher then went on to see if they could make 'family snakes' by writing the name of each family member on a flag, and sticking the flags into plasticine snakes, in sequence from the oldest to the youngest. Although the sequences had no clear order, Adam, for instance, grouped the 'nanny' flags together and insisted on one for the unborn baby at the other end of his snake.

Another student, Catherine Rigby, encouraged Year 5 children to make inferences about sources related to a Victorian topic. She gave them Victorian steel pens, a Victorian inkwell and a page from a copperplate copy book and asked them to practice writing the letters. They were enthusiastic. 'You're not like other teachers, you let us touch things without shouting at us.' Using the pens raised questions and led to discussion. One child spontaneously enacted how the monitors would have distributed the ink; this was information learned in a previous session. The children were voluntarily silent for a while, listening to the amazing noise of the nibs on the paper. They worked out how the ink was regulated by different nibs and wrote with uncharacteristic concentration. In another session, they were shown my grandmother's Victorian school time-table, with many hours allocated to needlework ('daylight permitting'), and to religious education, and they were shown a sampler. This led to a diverting discussion of religious beliefs, the amazing discovery that people could make their own clothes, and the observation that today some posters and stickers fulfil a similar purpose to that of sampler messages such as 'Charity begins at home'. They then went on to design and make their own samplers. This was a most surprising level of commitment from an extremely 'difficult' group of children.

Key stage 2, group 3, information technology data bases

The nature of a simple data-base programme was explained. It involves collecting information (records), with shared characteristics (fields), in order to look for patterns and trends. These can be recorded graphically as pie or bar charts, graphs or venn diagrams. We then considered the role of data bases in historical problem-solving. Firstly we listed the kinds of historical sources which could best be organised in this way:

(1)   street directories, census and parish records of births, deaths, age, sex, occupation, address;
(2)   other statistics relating to population (illness, height, diet);
(3)   trade figures (cattle sold at Smithfield, price, weight, numbers);
(4)   information about buildings or archaeological sites with some shared characteristics (e.g. plans of Roman villas, recording shape, size, hypercausts, mosaic pavements);
(5)   place-name endings in an area indicating time and date of settlement (Roman, Viking, Saxon).

Secondly, we discussed how such information could be investigated through asking questions about change and about the causes and effects of change and interpreting the findings in the light of incomplete evidence, uncertainty, probability and what is known of the period. Thirdly, strategies were considered for involving a whole class of children in constructing and interrogating a data base. Each child can collect information for at least one record, complete a 'record sheet' on paper, categorising the information in fields to ensure that s/he can structure the information in this way, then type the record onto the data base. Next, when all the information has been collected, each child can fill in a second sheet setting out a question and the correct format for asking this question of the data base. When children have the responses to their questions they can fill in the last part of the sheet, saying what inferences they can make from them. This tried and tested method ensures that everyone understands how to use the data base, and has equal access to creating and interrogating it in a short time, although the complexity of the questions and sophistication of the deductions can vary considerably.

After this introduction, the group divided to return with their findings at the end of the session. One group spent the morning in a nearby churchyard collecting information from gravestones to put into an 'Our Facts' program (Anita Straker. MEP/MESU Primary Project). The other interrogated a ready-made data base on the Croydon and Stockport work houses (Community Information Resource Project. Croydon Advisory Service), compiled by a group of teachers for use at a range of levels, and supported by accompanying documentary evidence. This could fit in well with a Victorian project. One interesting finding was that most of the inmates were described as paupers; one of the few other groups was 'female school teachers'. Deductions? Another finding was that there were few girls in the work house but a lot of young boys. Reasons?

Key stage 2, group 4, portraits and written sources

Students were given portraits of Elizabeth I and of Horatio Nelson, and conflicting written sources related to each portrait. They were asked how valid the portraits are, as historical evidence. The sources were:

(a) (i) The 'Ditchley' portrait of Elizabeth I *c.* 1592 painted by Marcus Gheeraerts.

(ii) Secondary sources explaining the circumstances in which it was painted and explaining the symbolism and imagery in the portrait: the purity of the eternally youthful virgin queen, the faery queen of pageantry, dominating a map of England and synonymous with it, banishing clouds and ushering in sunshine, her earring an armillary sphere symbolising the elements of God's created universe, and carrying a Protestant bible (Strong, 1987; Gittings, 1991).

(iii) Contemporary descriptions of Elizabeth at about this time:
Francesco Gradenigo 1596
'Short and ruddy in complexion, very strongly built'
M. de Maisse 1597
'old, her face being long and thin, her teeth yellow and decayed but her figure is fair and tall and graceful in whatever she does.'

Paul Hentzner 1598

'fair but wrinkled, her eyes small yet black and pleasant, her nose a little hooked... her hair an auburn colour but false...'

(b) (i) Portrait of Horatio Nelson painted after the Battle of the Nile.

(ii) Letter from Lord Nelson explaining how it had been commissioned, as a commemorative painting (Nelson Letters, 1971, Everyman, pp.195-7).

(iii) Secondary source describing the ferocity and bloodiness of the battle (Pocock, 1974, 1987).

It was interesting that history graduates in the group found this exercise difficult. Unlike children, they felt that they should have a vast body of knowledge to bring to bear on the problem, and several of them also said that as undergraduates they had never worked with sources; they had only compared accounts of professional historians. Some of them, for the first time, raised questions about the nature of history.

The students became very keen to try using written and pictorial sources with children. John Fusco gave Year 5 children working on land transport an 1845 poster advertising an omnibus service from Colne and Burnley to Blackpool. He observed the inferences they made, the strategies they used, how they developed their ideas through discussion, and the kind of questions which helped them to do this. Daniel recognised the selectivity of the evidence, 'It's called The Safety... They're trying to make people think it's safe to travel like that, but it might be dangerous...', Susan could make a valid inference about attitudes in society at the time. She didn't like seeing the horses whipped, but since 'they're showing them whipping them, nobody else must have minded'. The children were also very interested to argue about the meaning of the text. What was meant by 'obedient servants', by 'viz.', by 'Sea Bathing'? In another session, they were given an engraving by Doré of Ludgate Circus in 1872. Here, the children discussed the noise and crowds, and the speed of the traffic. They noticed that it was all either steam or horse-powered, and wondered how the street lamps worked. They noticed differences in the clothes of people in buses and carriages and the clothes of people on foot. They developed and contested each other's statements and recognised the incompleteness of the evidence: 'You can't tell what he's saying so you don't know if you're right.' They also noticed similarities with the present: 'I've seen a man in Tottenham Court Road with a placard like that.'

Key stage 2, group 5, the locality

Maps, directories, census records, engravings and photographs, newspaper accounts, buildings and street names

A range of records obtained from the local history library focused on three periods: the beginning, the middle and the end of the last century. They all referred to the immediate locality of the college. It was possible to trace changes. At the beginning of the century this was a rural environment with farms, streams and windmills. It was inhabited by whip makers, brewers and smiths and linked by the turnpike road to London and the coast. Then came the building of the railway at New Cross, with brick yards supporting the accompanying building development. This led to different social classes moving into the area by the end of the century ('independent gentlemen', chemists, grocers, engineers, surveyors, clerks, servants and labourers), whose places of origin were recorded in the census.

In giving such a range of documents to children, there would have to be clear groupings and precise questions. However, the adults selected their own enquiries. Some went off with cameras to take photographs from the same position today and compare similarities and differences. They found the site of the windmill at Thornville Street for example, and of the toll gate at the junction of Queens Road and New Cross Road. They stood where Lewisham High Road had once been photographed, splendid with carriages and gas lamps. Can we find the mews where the horses were kept? Is the gas fitting still on the wall?

Some went in search of 'older people' and asked them about the beginning of this century (they even returned with an elderly resident!). Some chose particular buildings and traced their occupants in a particular year last century, as a basis for supposing what life might have been like in the house then. Why did the 37-year-old wine merchant come from Spalding in Lincolnshire, offer lodgings to three scholars from Deptford, and to his 20-year-old wine merchant assistant, and employ a nursemaid of 17 from Market Rasen, at 44 Lewisham High Road in 1881? How did the 31-year-old chemist from Ireland come to live with his older French wife and his four infant children at number 56? What were their homes like, their clothes, their food, and what happened next? What did their road look like in the early photographs? Other students listed changes on three successive maps.

Linda Benton went on to do a similar exercise with Year 5 children, tracing changes in the locality of their school, through maps. She was amazed at how interested the children were and how well they were able to relate the observed environment to maps, to trace changes, and to relate maps to photographs, gravestone surveys, and written and oral accounts.

A one day workshop

The aim of this workshop was to introduce non-specialist primary school teachers to the thinking processes of historical problem-solving so that they could apply the National Curriculum attainment targets to KS 2 core study unit 1, Romans, Anglo-Saxons and Vikings in Britain, and so plan their own content and strategies for teaching this unit to children. A tall order in a short time!

To begin the day, three primary school history co-ordinators gave a brief overview of the Romans, Anglo-Saxons and Vikings, supported by maps, slides, and written primary and secondary sources. This gave the teachers basic information about where each of these groups came from, when and why, and told them something of their ways of life.

During the second part of the morning, teachers worked in groups to make time-lines for 100BC to 1000AD, to show different aspects of change. Two time-lines sequenced key events. (It was felt that this would give the opportunity to see that people have different reasons for what they select as 'key' events, that events cannot always be accurately dated, and that they represent different degrees of change.) The other time-lines showed clothes, buildings and domestic artefacts, agriculture and transport. Teachers were introduced to the idea of a time-line as a device for sequencing, for describing and explaining change, and the causes and effects of change, for observing and explaining similarities and differences and for cross-referencing change and different rates of change in different aspects of society. It was made clear that they can be made in different ways and interpreted at a range of levels. They may be made by individuals, or by a group; they may be small or span the length of a hall or corridor. They may be friezes on a wall, lines on a ceiling or 'linen lines' with pegs. They may be illustrated by writing, pictures or models, suspended from the ceiling, or displayed on bench tops. They may cover periods of different lengths. They may show sequence or precise dates; they may be to scale or not and are not necessarily linear.

Because time was short, teachers were asked to (photo)copy illustrations for their time-lines (whereas children would draw, or make models, or describe and explain in writing). A large variety of recently published materials was available: books, posters, postcards, slides, brochures about sites, museum publications. Teachers were introduced to this by using it for a particular purpose. They therefore became familiar with it, evaluated it, discussed it and cross-referenced it in double-quick time.

Everyone worked zealously! By the end of the morning, two large rooms were dripping with illustrations of changes in Britain from 100BC to 1000AD. As in any active learning situation, cueing from tutors was important, as the time-lines were being made; it was often important to explain that the problems arising were the essential nature of historical thinking. How far can you generalise from one example? What does one Viking longship in a museum represent? How far can you date change precisely? When did the Roman Empire end in Britain? Do all aspects of life change at the same rate? Did farming change under the Romans? What is development? Were the Romans more 'advanced' than the Saxons? Did these changes affect everybody? Did the Britons continue to live in Iron Age huts during the whole of the Roman period? Why did the Saxons become Christians? At first, people were confused and frustrated by such questions thrown up by the exercise.

Their presentation of the time-lines at the end of the session however, showed that they had begun to find the questions intriguing. The discussions they gave rise to were animated and teachers wanted to find out more. They had begun to understand what history is about.

The afternoon focused on the Roman period, since it was felt that people would be most confident about this. Teachers worked in groups to consider what different sources could tell us about the Romans: (secondary school classics courses provide useful documentation).

(i) Written evidence: (a) description of Caesar's landing in Britain, 26 August 55BC (De Bello Gallico IV.23)
(b) description of Boudicca from Tacitus' Annals XIV 29–34.

(ii) Roman pottery found in the area, borrowed from a local museum. The curator explained where it was thought to have come from and its status. Rather coarse roof tiles, for example, represent a building of status in Roman Britain.

    (iii) Plan of the Roman Villa at Lullingstone.
    (iv) Map of South East England in Roman times showing roads, towns and forts, tribes, tracks, iron workings, wooded areas and escarpments.
    (v) Detail of frieze from the Great Dish, Mildenhall. British Museum slide PRB 47.
    (vi) Shield boss found in the River Tyne (BM slide).

There was much discussion about what could be worked out, and also the limitations of each of the sources. People were surprised by the immediacy of the description of Boudicca:

> She was a huge woman, with a piercing gaze and strident voice. A mane of chestnut hair hung below her waist. Round her neck was a great golden torque. She wore a full, flowing tartan dress, and over it a thick cloak fastened by a brooch. She grasped a spear to terrify everyone.

How true is Tacitus' description? There were lively arguments about the veracity of Caesar's account of his landing.

In the final session of the day, teachers were given the Statements of Attainment for each of the attainment targets and discussed how they related to the day's work. Then they were given a selection of formats for planning a study unit, relating resources to activities and assessment, which they filled in over the following few weeks. The range of different plans which they submitted and which were collated as a shared resource, for interpreting the attainment targets in relation to the content of this study unit, were encouraging in their variety.

It has been impressive to see the determination and goodwill with which teachers are trying to implement the National Curriculum for history. The best advice seems to be to concentrate on selected study units; do not try to do them all in equal depth. Within a study unit get an over-view of key events and changes by introducing time-lines and time vocabulary, and asking questions about why things changed. Then select a few examples of key evidence, preferably related to a visit, which can be used as clues to find out more about the period.

CHAPTER 6

The National Curriculum and Action Research

As has been said earlier in this book, little is known about the levels of historical thinking which primary school children are capable of achieving or about how best to promote these or how to assess them. The National Curriculum is a considered, but no more than an initial, attempt to provide a structure for promoting development in historical thinking. However, research has suggested that promoting and monitoring children's development in history is particularly difficult because of interdependent influences: the nature of the evidence, the questions asked of it, and the teaching strategies used. The sequence and appropriateness of the Statements of Attainment in the National Curriculum depends on the given evidence and on the particular questions asked. It is possible to put events in sequence, to differentiate between the real and the fictitious, and to communicate information from a historical source (all level 1 statements), at any level. This is what professional historians do. Furthermore, the attainment targets themselves may well prove not to be the best definition of the inter-acting processes of historical thinking. Therefore, any refined development in our understanding of children's historical thinking which will inform good practice will depend on building up banks of shared information about what children can do. Blyth, in *Making the Grade in Primary Humanities* (1990) emphasised the need for teachers to meet, both horizontally across their age range, and vertically in cross-phase groups to share ideas, support each other, plan, discuss and evaluate. They may, for example, devise shared teaching plans for a number of schools for the same age range for a unit of study, or construct a specific assessment exercise and compare the extent to which children react similarly. They may devise an assessment method and use it with different age groups, or combine to plan a local study unit.

This chapter will consider research done over two consecutive years as a class teacher of Year 4 children (Cooper, 1991), partly because it may offer some insights into teaching strategies and their effects, and also to encourage busy class teachers to consider action research as an inbuilt part of their approach to National Curriculum history. In the light of teachers' findings, the National Curriculum may ultimately be modified in the way that both the National Working Group Final Report (1990, pp. 175–6), and the Secretary of State in his speech to AMMA (1990) advocated.

The research design

This investigates the hypothesis that young children can become involved in historical problem-solving, that there is a sequence in the early stages of their thinking which can be evaluated, that teaching strategies are significant in developing children's historical thinking, and that consistent teaching strategies can accelerate this development.

The research was undertaken in two primary schools in an outer suburb of south London. The following extracts of a discussion amongst eight-year-old children, about the Iron Age chalk horse at Uffington in Berkshire, give an introductory flavour of the study. It is interesting to compare them with the definition of a horse required by Mr Gradgrind, in the introduction to this book.

> 'It looks like a bird.'
> 'It's a horse.'
> 'They could draw horses.'
> 'So they had horses.'
> 'They were hard workers . . . skilful . . . artistic . . . .'
>
> 'There must be a lot of chalk near the surface.'
> 'So there wouldn't be trees like oak trees here – not many trees.'
> 'They could live on the chalk – it's well-drained – the water would run away.'
> 'The soil would be thin – easy to plough.'
>
> 'Whatever tools they used, they must have been able to dig down into the ground to get to the chalk.'
> 'It must have taken a long time to make – maybe centuries.'
> 'They were hard workers . . . skilful . . . artistic . . .'.
> 'They co-operated.'
> 'They lived in a community.'

'It's not an ordinary horse. It's much different from the ones we see.'
'It must be a special one or they wouldn't go to all that trouble.'
'It's probably a symbol for something – a clue.'
'To bring a good harvest?'
'A symbol of strength?'
'To an enemy? Perhaps the horse brought bad luck so they stayed away.'
'Perhaps if someone was ill they prayed to it. It gave them power when they were ill.'
'Or perhaps they just did it for fun.'
'Maybe they danced around it – or put fires on it and burnt something – maybe for the chief's birthday.'
'I don't think they had birthdays.'
'But they had beliefs and ceremonies.'
'Customs.'

These children discuss the geology and the social organisation needed to make the horse, its practical and symbolic significance. They follow through and weigh each other's points. They synthesise them using abstract concepts: co-operate, community, ceremonies, beliefs, customs. They make a distinction between what they know and what they can only speculate about.

Two 'experimental' classes of Year 4 children were taught during consecutive years using carefully defined and documented teaching strategies and compared with a control group in another school taught by an experienced teacher using his own methods. The three groups were initially compared for ability by analyses of variance and co-variance using NFER Non-Verbal Reasoning Test BD as covariate. All three groups were taught the same 4 units of history: the Stone Age, the Iron Age, the Romans and the Saxons, each unit lasting half a term. Each unit was taught within an integrated curriculum with a historical focus. About two hours each week were spent specifically on history.

The teaching strategies for the experimental groups involved discussion of key evidence, differentiating between what you could know 'for certain', what reasonable 'guesses' you could make, and what you 'would like to know' about the evidence. The discussion involved selected key concepts of different levels of abstraction (e.g. arrow, weapon, defence). Each unit of study involved one visit to a local area where there was evidence of settlement at each period and one 'further afield' visit to extend beyond the locality. For example, the Stone Age 'further afield' visit was to Grimes Graves, and the Roman one was to Lullingstone Roman Villa.

Table 6.1: *Evidence used in written and oral evidence tests*

Unit	Test 1 Artefact	Test 2 Picture	Test 3 Diagram	Test 4 Map	Test 5 Writing
1	Slide. Palaeolithic flint hard axes c. 200,000BC Museum of London. Slide OL91	Slide. Font de Gaume Lascaux. Ray Delvert S. Lot.	Stone circle. The Druids Circle. Caernarvon. Stone circles of the British Isles. A. Burle	Map showing site of neolithic artefacts on North Downs	Petroglyphics from 'How Writing Began' Macdonald
2	Bronze helmet (1BC) Slide BM	Uffington Horse photos	Little Woodbury, Iron Age house plan Wilts. In Cunliffe, R.K. 1974	Lynchets of Iron Age Fields Butser Hill, Hants.	Strabo 1.4.2. Description of British exports
3	Shield boss found in River Tyne. Slide BM.	Detail from frieze of great dish, Mildenhall Slide BM PRB 47	Villa plan Chedworth, Gloucs.	Roman roads across South Downs	Tacitus Annales XII 31–40 Boudicca Revolt
4	Replica of Sceptre. Sutton Hoo ship burial. BM Slide MZ 18	Illuminated manuscript of Harvest made by BM F21985	Plan Saxon church Cirencester	Saxon settlements in Surrey	Beowulf slays Grendel Penguin 1973 trans 824–838

At the end of each unit, all three groups took five written 'evidence tests' which each lasted about half-an-hour on consecutive days. In each unit these consisted of five different types of evidence about which children had to make inferences: an artefact (or slide of one), a picture, a diagram, a map and written evidence. The aim was to investigate whether they found 'concrete' evidence more difficult to interpret than more abstract maps and written evidence. A list of evidence used is given in Table 6.1.

The experimental groups were also given an oral 'evidence test'. The children made a tape-recording of a discussion of each piece of evidence in small groups. During the first year the discussions were led by the teacher, and during the following year, no adult was present.

In addition, the second experimental group was given a story-writing test. They were given a piece of evidence related to the topic which was concerned with religion, beliefs, myth and ritual, so that it invited the children to piece together their knowledge into a coherent picture of the past and to attempt to consider and explain the beliefs and ideas of the period.

An assessment scheme on a ten-point scale was devised for the evidence tests. This was constructed from patterns in the development of deductive reasoning defined in cognitive psychology and in previous research relating this to history. It is not possible to quote it in detail, but it ranges from:

level 1 – illogical;
level 2 – incipient logic not clearly expressed;
level 3 – restatement of information given;
levels 4 and 5 – one or two statements going beyond the information given;
level 6 – an attempted sequential statement inadequately expressed;
levels 7 and 8 – one or two logical sequential statements, where the second statement is based on the first, connected by 'therefore' or 'because';
levels 9 and 10 – a synopsis of previous points, using an abstract concept.

For example, given a map of an area of the North Downs where Stone Age implements have been found, a typical level 3 answer is 'There are clay areas, and chalk areas and steep slopes,' (which are given on the map). A level 4 statement is 'They had rivers to get water from.' An example of a level 8 statement is 'Chalky ground is not wet, therefore the tools are found there because Stone Age people could live there. And they were near a river, so they could get water to drink.' An example of a level 10 statement refers to a diagram of an Iron Age hut: 'They had huts. Therefore they could build huts. They had vegetation. Therefore they had materials to make huts. They had houses, shelter and stores.'

A system was devised for analysing group discussions and recording points made using this scale by dividing a page horizontally into 10 sections, recording synopses of points under levels and mapping the children's development of each other's arguments (Diagram 6.2). This analysis could then be transferred to a variety of other diagrammatic forms (Diagrams 6.3 and 6.4).

The story-writing test was assessed using a scale based on Ashby and Lee (1987) and Piaget (1932). This ranged from no awareness of ideas, beliefs and values and so no attempt to explain them, through inter-mediate levels when children mention symbolic artefacts in passing, but do not reflect on the ideas they may represent, and finally to an attempt to suggest the significance of symbols.

The findings

The relationship between interpreting evidence and the development of historical imagination and empathy – implications for story-writing

In analysing the written 'evidence tests' unit 1, The Stone Age, it became apparent that the deductive reasoning scale reflected levels of argument, but did not reflect a difference in the quality of the answers of the control and experimental groups. The experimental groups' answers were more varied and more closely derived from the evidence, while the control group often simply repeated given information which was not rooted in the evidence. The control group displayed more anachronisms, and stereotypes and the assumption that people in the past were simple. Given a plan of a stone circle, for example, the experimental children suggested a variety of possible purposes (KM 'reconed it was for war dances, trading flint, praying'), and they suggested how it may have been made. The control group answers were dominated by repeating received information about 'magic oak trees', 'Druids in white cloaks', and 'scarey magic'.

This difference in quality was examined further in unit 2. Answers were grouped under Collingwood's (1939) three categories of historical enquiry: How was it made? How was it used? What did it mean to people at the time? The following analysis of the experimental groups' responses to the 'Waterloo Helmet' evidence (British Museum slide) shows how they considered each of these questions (although they had not been explicitly asked to do so). They had been asked 'what do you know for certain? What reasonable guesses can you make, and what would you like to know?'. Their answers suggest that it is through asking questions of evidence that children gradually learn to consider and attempt to explain the viewpoints of people who lived in other times. It also seems likely that the experimental groups were better able to do this because they had been taught through discursive teaching strategies which encouraged them to make a range of valid suppositions about evidence.

Experimental groups

Written test

I How Was it Made?

HC Exp 1. Qu 1 NVR 97
'They had metals . . . they could make things.'

JG Exp 2. Qu 1 NVR 120
'They could smelt iron and bronze . . . they had a furnace for getting iron out of rock . . . .'

IW Exp 1. Qu 1 NVR 123
'They had charcoal to separate metal from ore.'

ML Exp 1. Qu 3 NVR 102
'I would like to know if the horns were hollow, because if they are it would be lighter.'

RL Exp 1. Qu 1 NVR 107
'They must have had good minds to remember things . . . . They knew how to get to learn.'

Discussion tapes

JH Exp 2. NVR 100
'They made it carefully with the right kind of metals. Certainly they used a mould and little rivets.'

MF Exp 2. NVR 129
'They had the right tools to shape the metal.'

NH Exp 1. NVR 105
'They could print patterns on it. They had a habit of putting circles on their working.'

GP Exp 1. NVR 133
'They had weapons – shields and swords too. At the British Museum, I copied a sword with a bronze hilt.'

II What was it used for?

(a) For protection in battle

HG Exp 1. Qu 2 NVR 129
'They wore it to protect their heads . . . they had fights. They made it . . . they made weapons. They had wars.'

MF Exp 2. Qu 3 NVR 129
'I would like to know how they got the idea of armour, and why did they fight?'

NH Exp 1. NVR 105
'They invented things. They knew how to smelt metal.'
Exp 1.
'It's got horns. It looks fierce – like an ox that could kill. Like a Stone-Age hunter's deer antlers – to hide in the bushes. The pattern could show what side you were on so you didn't kill your own men.'

'They fought for food. If there was a bad winter and cattle died . . . to steal another tribe's cattle, or to cut another tribe's corn if they didn't have enough.'

(b) As a ceremonial symbol or trophy

KC Exp 2. Qu 2 NVR 111
'It might be made for a chief . . . he would wear it at ceremonies to look special.'

NH Exp 1. NVR 105
'Maybe the more metal you had it showed how high up you were. They'd start with a bracelet 'til they were all covered in metal then they'd be a chief.'

NH Exp 1. Qu 2 NVR 105
'They might have used it at chariot races . . . they might have had it as a medal. They might have liked beautiful things and had it as an ornament.'

Exp 2.
'It may have been awarded for extreme bravery in battle. Or in a contest for new warriors. Maybe they had races and contests, and the armour was awarded for use in a battle.'

SH Exp 1. Qu 2 NVR 104
'It might have been for a goddess.'

Exp 1.
'If they found other things in the River Thames, they may be offerings to a water goddess, to thank her for water to drink.'

(c) *A commodity to trade*
ES Exp 1. Qu 3 NVR 129
'How did the archaeologists come to find it, because it would tell me if it was made there, or if they traded them.'

Exp 2.
'They could have traded it for helmets made in another land. Or maybe for metal to make more weapons. Maybe, as we learned in a lesson, Julius Caesar wrote they used rods of equal weight, or coins, to trade. They could have traded it for bronze or iron – probably for metal of some kind.'

RL Exp 1. Qu 3 NVR 107
'And was there one people in the place who made them? ... if he did he would be rich.'

III What did it mean to the people who wore it?
PC Exp 2. Qu 1 NVR 114
'They were not afraid of going into battle ... they looked fierce ... they put fierce patterns on them.'

Exp 2.
'The patterns make it look sort of mysterious – they look like flowers ... it might mean something like "long live our tribe" or "our tribe is the horse tribe". Or special orders from their God. Or a magic helmet to help them in battle. Or the wearer's name. Or to describe the wearer – how good he was at hunting or fighting.'

ML Exp 1. Qu 2 NVR 102
'I guess it had a kind of strap.'

KL Exp 1. Qu 3 NVR 107
'Did they make different shapes and sizes, because it would have to fit . . . ?'

DS Exp 1. Qu 3 NVR 88
'I would like to know what it felt like to put it on. It must have been heavy to handle.'

Exp 2.
'The strips at the side probably had vines or strings attached to hold it on to the wearer . . . they must have put something on it to make it shine . . . maybe it was measure for the wearer's head.'

Exp 1.
'It's so heavy they probably took it with them and put it on when they got there.'

When the study was planned, it had seemed that making deductions from evidence and historical imagination were different and discrete aspects of historical thinking, and for this reason, separate evidence and story-writing tests were devised. However, analysis of the evidence tests suggested that historical imagination develops through making valid suppositions about how things were made and used in the past and so considering what they may have meant to people at the time, and that this is the vehicle through which historical empathy may develop. Since historical imagination and historical empathy are defined in innumerable ways, their relationship as defined in this study is given in Diagram 6.1.

This has implications for story-writing in history. Analysis of the story-writing tests showed that while children enjoy trying to reconstruct the past through story-writing, and that they do consider and try to explain ideas and beliefs different from their own, their knowledge is limited and they are immature so that they are unable to take a holistic view of society (Furth, 1980). In writing stories, imagination is not necessarily tied closely to evidence, and interpretations of evidence do not have to be argued as they do in discussion. Therefore, anachronisms and misunderstandings are more likely to go unchecked. (Historical fiction is very difficult to write.) In the Stone Age unit, for example, the children were given a postcard of the Barnack Grave, 1800 BC (BM PR 34) with drawings of the grave goods,

Diagram 6.1: *Relationship between historical imagination and historical empathy as defined in this study*

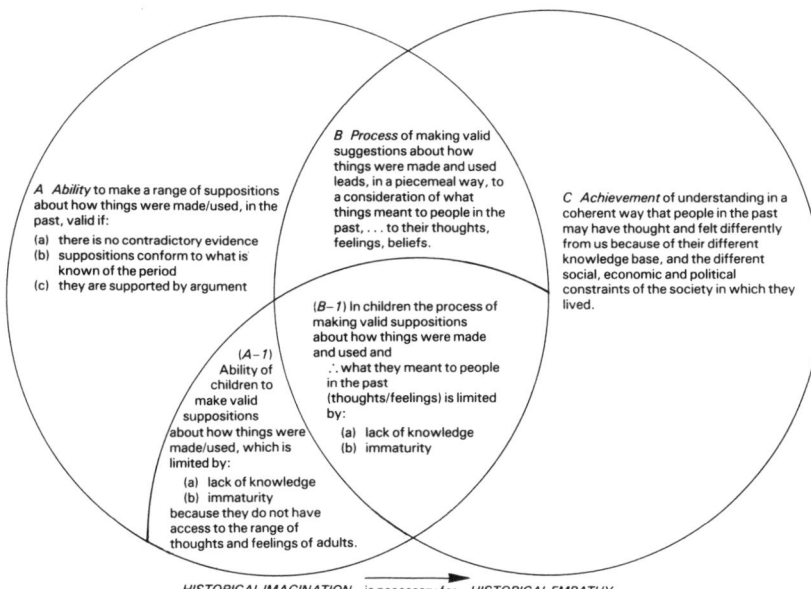

A Ability to make a range of suppositions about how things were made/used, in the past, valid if:
(a) there is no contradictory evidence
(b) suppositions conform to what is known of the period
(c) they are supported by argument

B Process of making valid suggestions about how things were made and used leads, in a piecemeal way, to a consideration of what things meant to people in the past, . . . to their thoughts, feelings, beliefs.

C Achievement of understanding in a coherent way that people in the past may have thought and felt differently from us because of their different knowledge base, and the different social, economic and political constraints of the society in which they lived.

(A–1)
Ability of children to make valid suppositions about how things were made/used, which is limited by:
(a) lack of knowledge
(b) immaturity
because they do not have access to the range of thoughts and feelings of adults.

(B–1) In children the process of making valid suppositions about how things were made and used and
∴ what they meant to people in the past (thoughts/feelings) is limited by:
(a) lack of knowledge
(b) immaturity

HISTORICAL IMAGINATION is necessary for *HISTORICAL EMPATHY*

a walrus or whale-bone pendant, a bronze dagger, a wristguard and a decorated pot, and asked to write a story called 'The Death of the Archer'. About one third of the children explained this with a story which attached no significance to the grave goods. 'An archer was doing pottery. He might have been shaping it with a dagger. The spear was to protect him. Someone came to the door and threw a flint at him and he fell on the fire.' Others may regard the objects as significant, but they did not reflect on why. Children are caught in a time-warp and see the archer die. 'They bury him with all his things, a bone necklace, a bronze dagger and a large pot,' or the archer was killed in a battle. 'His wife put some of his things around the fire before they burned him.'

At the highest level of response to emerge stories contained more detailed description of artefacts and more complicated narrative: 'In a village there lived a boy called Balloo. He was learning to do archery. Every three weeks he would get a feather. One day he was given a brilliant surprise – a wristguard; the chance to be a hunter with all the others . . .'. However there was no attempt to explain the significance of the grave goods or the ideas they represented.

It is not suggested that children should never be asked to write stories about the past, but 'Imagine you were...' should be treated with caution. If they are asked to do this, children need to be shown how to relate a reconstruction to evidence. Sylvester (1989) showed how a seven-year-old can use knowledge based on evidence from a pictorial source to write a story about the bubonic plague and the fire, and how a 12-year-old can use directories, plans and logs to write about a day in the life of a Victorian boy. Little (1989) gives two examples of story-writing by 10-year-olds about Spain's conquest of the Inca. In one, a different way of life, hierarchy and ceremony are understood and factual information has been translated into a reconstruction, while in the other, knowledge is thrown in without a sense of time or detail.

Assessing levels of argument

The written evidence tests

In the written evidence tests, the children were given an answer paper which they were told to fill in, pretending they were archaeologists reporting on the evidence (the example shows how Andrew filled in his 'archaeologist's' report on the petroglyphics at the end of the Stone Age unit). Answer papers were laid out to encourage the highest levels of response, based on the 10 point scale described on p. 131. They made a distinction between 'knowing', 'guessing', and 'not knowing', and encouraged children to make two statements for each of these categories, to follow each with a sequential argument and to write a 'conclusion'.

However, it was frequently necessary to look for the underlying logic of the thinking processes behind an answer in order to assess the level of thinking. Often this was obscured by poor spelling or handwriting. An answer may span several levels and would then be scored on the basis of the highest scoring statements within the answer and lower levels ignored. The logic of the answer does not always correspond to the divisions on the paper, so that the statements need to be carefully considered.

The oral evidence tests

Diagram 6.2 shows how the oral evidence tests were also analysed on the 10 point scale. These synopses refer to the written evidence used in the Iron Age unit (Strabo 1.4.2).

139

NAME Andrew   DATE 6.12.85

UNIT ONE   THE STONE AGES

EVIDENCE writing

What do you know FOR CERTAIN from this evidence?		Level 9
they communicated	**Therefore** they made signs for communicating	**Conclusion** they needed other people
they draw	**Therefore** They had thing to draw with	

What reasonable GUESSES can you make about it?		Level 8
they may of had spcshells thing to do writing with	**Therefore**	**Conclusion** they might of had spcshell hunting signs
I think it had a meaning	**Therefore** It migh of taken them a long time to get the writing	

What would you LIKE TO KNOW about it?		Level 6
What it ment	**Because** then we could make little word	**Conclusion**
had they got to know wHat the signs ment	**Because** then we could do stone age writing.	

Diagram 6.2: *Synopsis of led and unled discussion showing how it is represented as a diagram*

Unit 2 Test 5 led discussion experimental group 1: JW, JB, GP, MS, BK, CB. T = Teacher

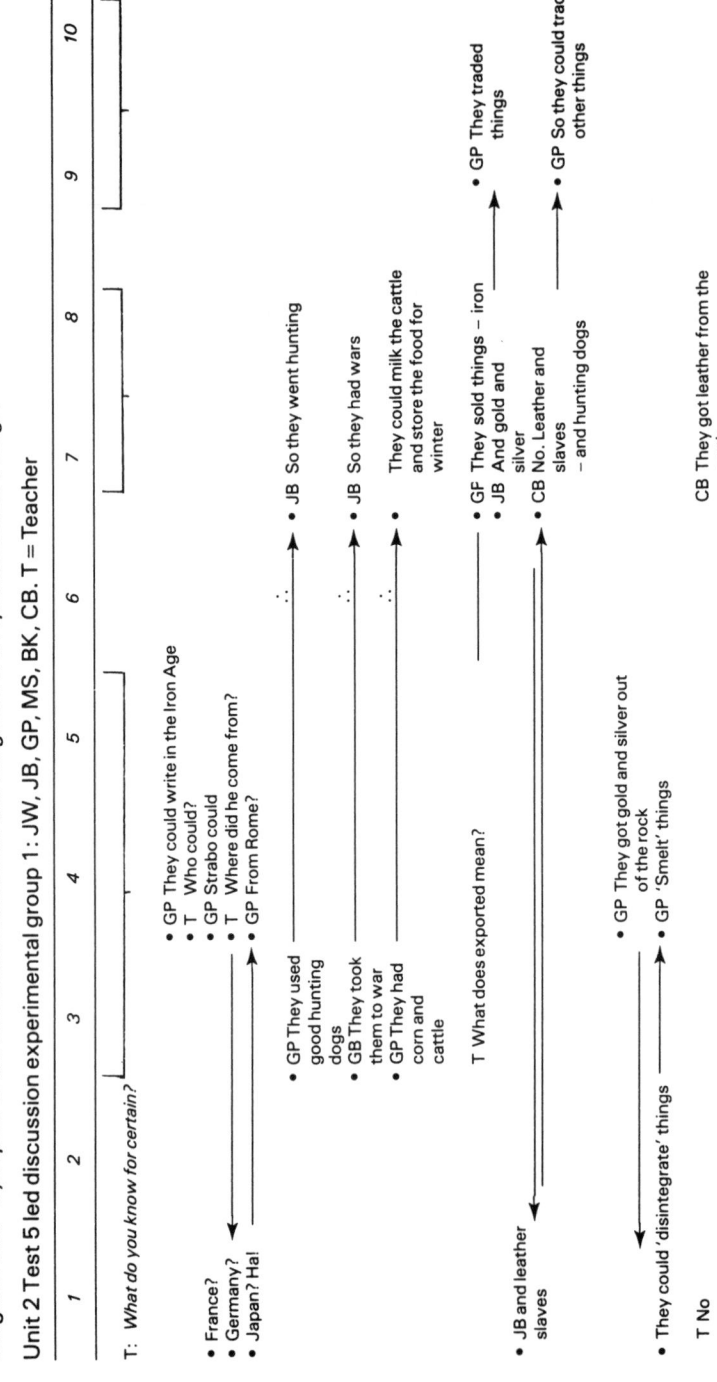

Diagram 6.2: *Cont*

Unit 2 Test 5 led discussion

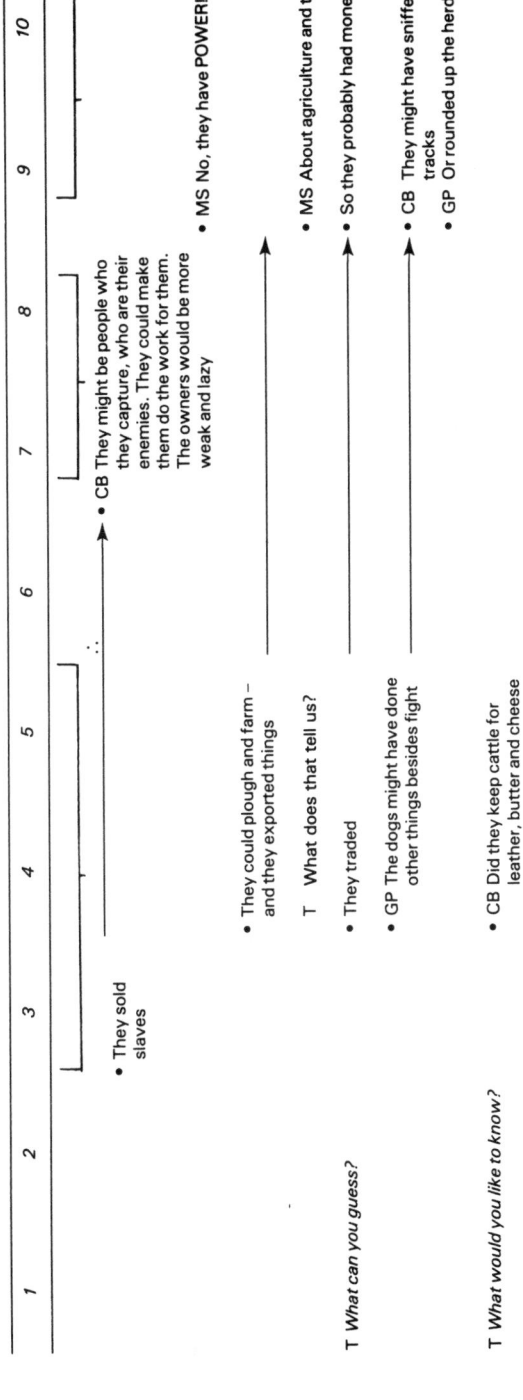

	1	2	3	4	5	6	7	8	9	10

• They sold slaves

• CB They might be people who they capture, who are their enemies. They could make them do the work for them. The owners would be more weak and lazy

• MS No, they have POWER!

• They could plough and farm – and they exported things

T What does that tell us?

• MS About agriculture and trade

T *What can you guess?*

• They traded

• So they probably had money

• GP The dogs might have done other things besides fight

• CB They might have sniffed tracks
• GP Or rounded up the herd

T *What would you like to know?*

• CB Did they keep cattle for leather, butter and cheese or for ploughing?
• GP Not actual *cows* for ploughing. They used oxen. They were stronger

T *Is there anything else you would like to know?* Unanimous 'no!'

Diagram 6.2: *Cont: Synopsis of led and unled discussions showing how it is represented as a diagram*

Unit 2 Test 5 writing (Strabo 1.4.2.) Exp. Group 2. Unled discussion LW, JF, KB, FB, MS

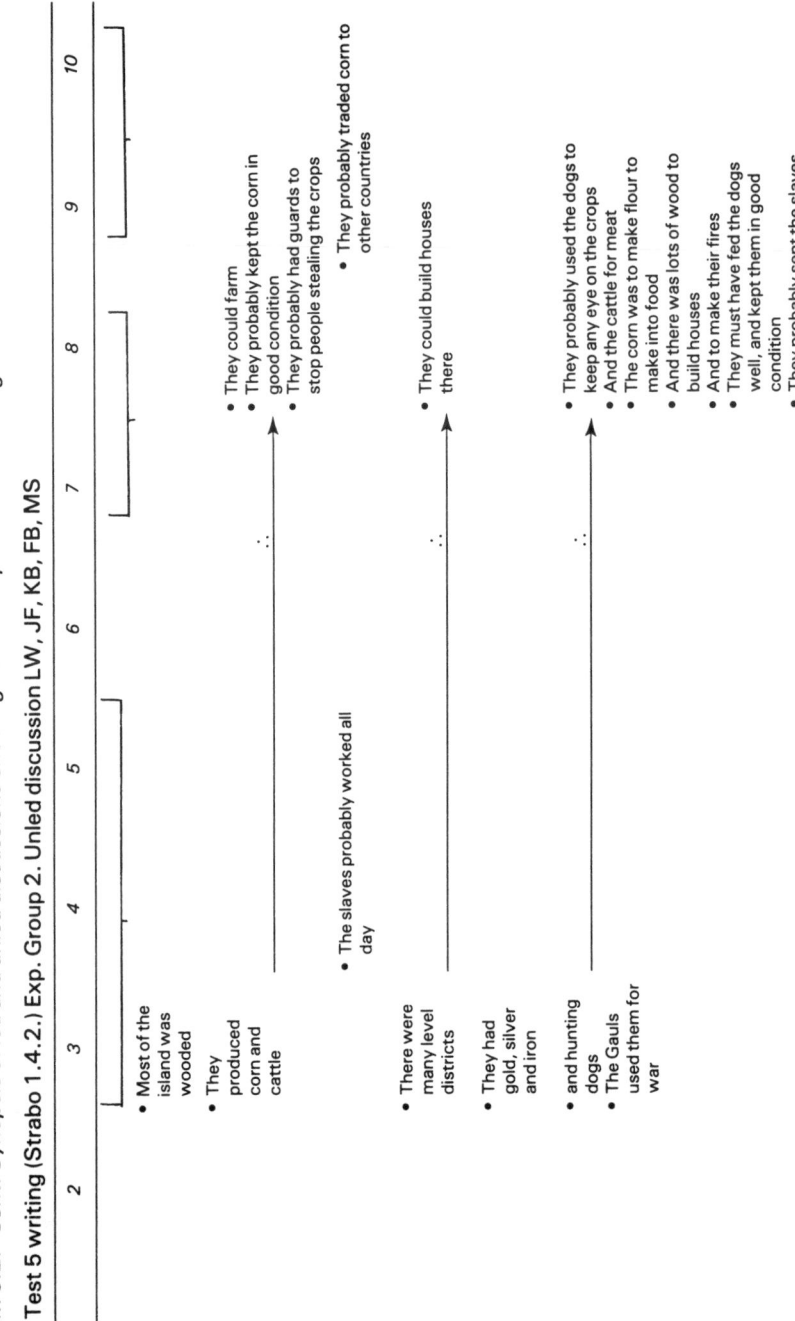

1	2	3	4	5	6	7	8	9	10

- Most of the island was wooded
- They produced corn and cattle

- They could farm
- They probably kept the corn in good condition
- They probably had guards to stop people stealing the crops
- They probably traded corn to other countries

- The slaves probably worked all day

- There were many level districts

- They could build houses there

- They had gold, silver and iron

- and hunting dogs
- The Gauls used them for war

- They probably used the dogs to keep any eye on the crops
- And the cattle for meat
- The corn was to make flour to make into food
- And there was lots of wood to build houses
- And to make their fires
- They must have fed the dogs well, and kept them in good condition
- They probably sent the slaves out to do the hunting.

Diagram 6.3: *Led and unled discussions*

Unit 2, Test 5, writing. Strabo (1.4.2.)

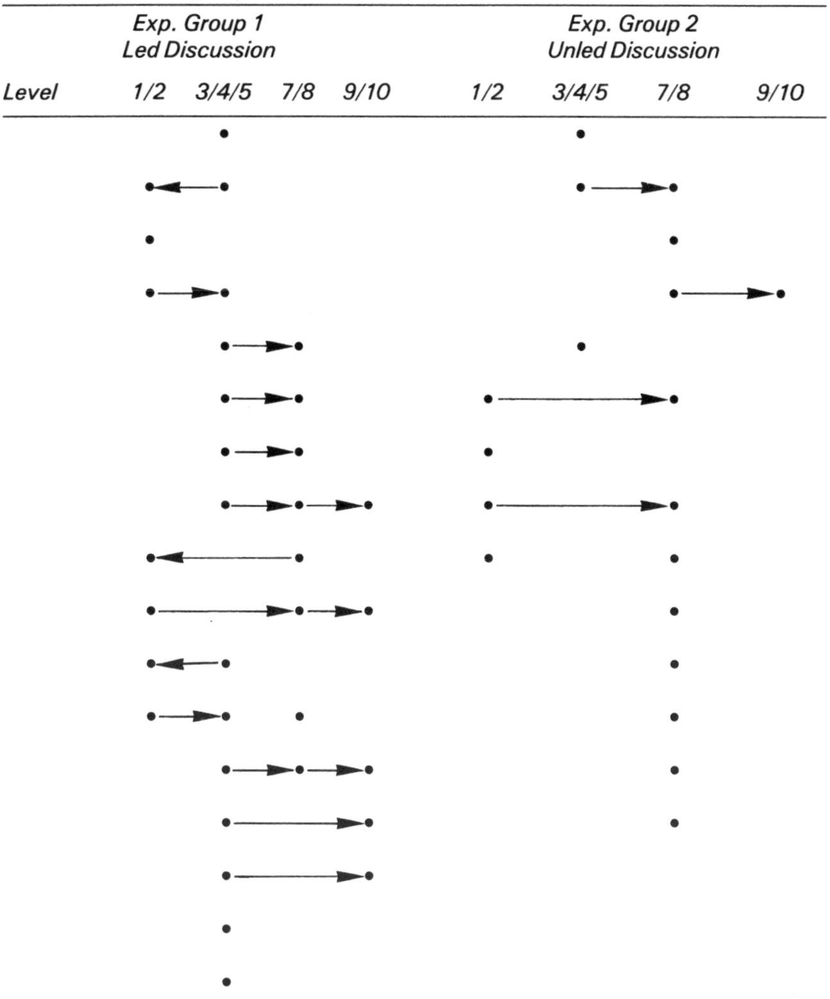

	Exp. Group 1 Led Discussion				Exp. Group 2 Unled Discussion			
Level	1/2	3/4/5	7/8	9/10	1/2	3/4/5	7/8	9/10

Points made at each level in led and unled discussions

Led Discussion		Unled Discussion	
level 1/2	5 points	level 1/2	4 points
level 3/4/5	13 points	level 3/4/5	3 points
level 7/8	8 points	level 7/8	11 points
level 9/10	5 points	level 9/10	1 point
Total:	31 points	Total:	19 points

Most of the island is level and well-wooded, but there are many hilly districts. It produces corn, cattle, gold, silver and iron. They are all exported, together with leather, slaves and good hunting dogs. The Gauls use these dogs, and their own, for war as well.

Diagram 6.3 shows how the levels were then mapped, so that they could be transferred to tables, to compare levels of argument achieved in individual written answers and in group discussion, over the four periods of study.

Making a distinction between 'knowing' and 'supposing'

In the written 'evidence tests' the children were asked three questions about each piece of evidence: question one, what do you know for certain? question two, what reasonable 'guesses' can you make? question three, what would you like to know? It is interesting that they were able to make these distinctions. Analysis of the unled discussion tapes, where they were not specifically asked to differentiate between knowing, guessing and not knowing, nevertheless show the discussions dominated by probability words (could be, maybe, unlikely, I wonder, what you think?). The children occasionally make certainty statements. 'They (the axe heads), were all chipped and smoothed' and sometimes these are challenged by other children: 'It's got two heads.' (cave painting). 'That could be a tail.' 'Bit thick for a tail.'

The unled groups also sometimes mention things that they would like to know. 'It must have been for some reason?' 'How do you think they made the banks?'

It is interesting that in the written 'evidence tests' the children were able to make 'certainty' statements, and reasonable guesses (questions 1 and 2) with almost equal ease. The graph (Figure 6.1) based on analysis of variance tests to compare groups, questions and types of evidence in each unit, shows a significant difference between the types of question, with question 3 (what would you like to know?), by far the most difficult. The Sheffé test of multiple comparison shows the difference between the first two questions and question 3 to be significant. These children then are able to make a distinction between knowing and valid suppositions, and they find both types of inference equally easy, but they find it far harder to say what they 'would like to know' about evidence.

Although these results were statistically significant, there were exceptions to the main effects. There were significant interactions

Figure 6.1: *Graph showing means of scores for questions 1, 2 and 3 for units 1, 2 and 4*

(Unit 3 was taught and tested, but the results were not analysed due to shortage of time.)
The marking scale is outlined on p. 131.

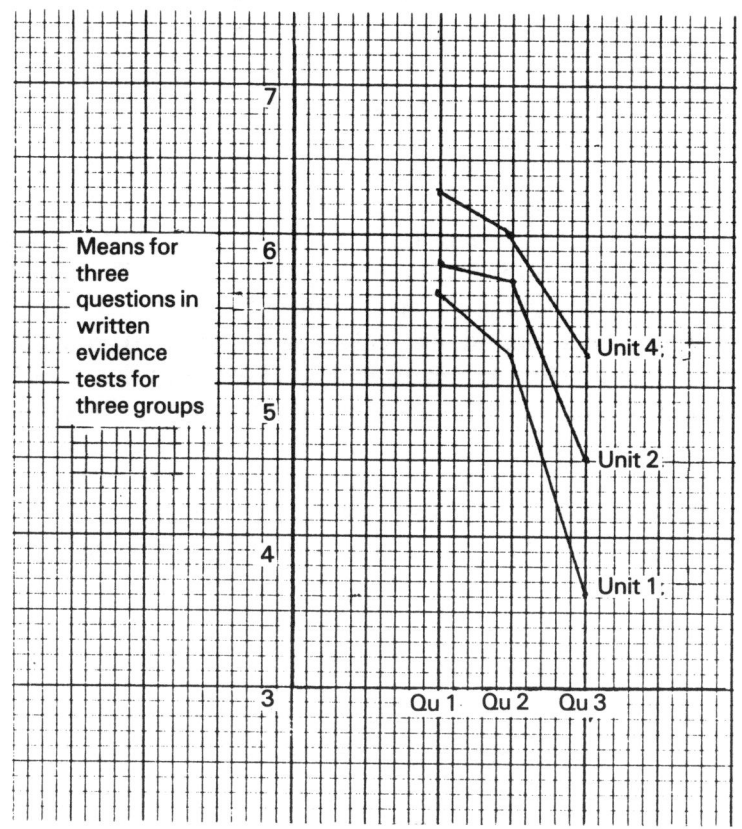

Question 1   What do you know FOR CERTAIN, from this evidence?
Question 2   What REASONABLE GUESSES can you make from this evidence?
Question 3   What WOULD YOU LIKE TO KNOW about this evidence?

between the questions and types of evidence. In unit 1, for example, there was little difference in difficulty between knowing and guessing about the cave painting, the plan of the stone circle, or the map. This is not surprising because not much is known about how these things were made or used or what they meant to Stone Age people, even by archaeologists, so there are fertile opportunities for reasonable guesses. On the other hand, it was easier to make certainty statements about axe-heads because these are central to a study of the Stone Age. The experimental groups had three lessons on tools and weapons and had seen them made at Grimes Graves. This is important because it shows how statistically significant main effects are blurred by other variables, by a particular example of a type of evidence, by interest and by motivation.

There do however, seem to be implications for teachers, in the general finding, that children are equally able to say what they know, and to make reasonable suggestions, but find it difficult to say what they 'would like to know'. It suggests that children of this age do not need to be restricted to repeating 'facts' and that they are able to become actively involved in historical problem-solving. They can learn to control their own thinking, and become increasingly aware of what constitutes a valid supposition. This is an important staging post on the way to true historical understanding. However, 'what would you like to know?' is a question with an unknown starting point, and is too open. It does not encourage children to control their own investigation. This is significant because children are frequently told to 'find out about . . .', particularly at the ends of chapters in history books, assuming this encourages motivation and independent learning. These tests suggest that such a question is too unstructured.

Different types of evidence

The study set out to investigate whether children find it easier to make deductions about artefacts and pictures than about more abstract evidence, diagrams, maps and written sources. The relationship between groups, questions and evidence in each unit was statistically analysed using analyses of variance. The findings are shown in Figure 6.2.

Although in unit 1 there was a significant difference between the levels of response to the five types of evidence, and the children found the diagram and the map the most difficult, it is interesting that by unit 2, and again in unit 4, there was no significant difference in their ability to interpret 'concrete' and 'abstract' evidence. This is not to suggest that it is not very important for children to be introduced to artefacts and pictures (which are, at the very least, stimulating sources), but rather that if they are given more abstract evidence as well, as part of a continuum and have learned to discuss evidence, they can interpret abstract sources equally well. This seems to be because, having learned

Figure 6.2: *Graph showing means of scores for five types of evidence for units 1, 2 and 4*

(Unit 3 was taught and tested, but the results were not analysed due to shortage of time.)
The marking scale is outlined on p. 131.

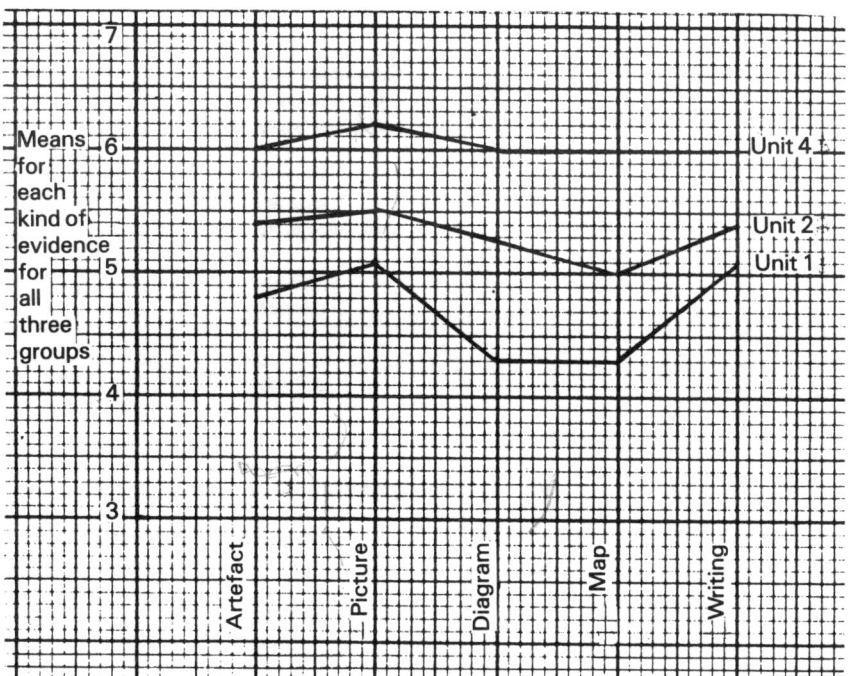

how to discuss evidence and the kinds of responses required, they can relate abstract evidence to 'concrete' evidence – maybe through visits to sites or museums. The experimental groups had visited Grimes Graves, the British Museum and local sites, and related these to maps, geology, vegetation and relief. They could therefore draw on these experiences in interpreting, for example, the Stone Age axe-heads, the Waterloo Helmet, the plans of the stone circle, the Iron Age hut, and the maps.

Their level of response depends, not on the level of abstraction of the evidence, but on language, on concepts and on argument, because remains of the past are only evidence to the extent that they can tell us about the people who made and used them. Children need to experience physical evidence, and to learn to discuss it, if it is to have meaning for them. They are then able to transfer this process to new evidence, and to more abstract evidence.

148

Figure 6.3: *The taught concepts in unit 2 used in discussion tapes*

1 cm. represents the use of the concept in one evidence test on one or more occasions

■ represents led discussion groups (Exp 1)
▨ represents unled discussion groups (Exp 2)

Led (Exp 1)		11	*Unled* (Exp 2)		
Concrete	9		Concrete	9	
Abstract	9		Abstract	8	
Superordinate	10		Superordinate	1	

This bar chart shows how both the led and unled groups used their taught vocabulary in unit 2 discussions and, when appropriate, used concepts learned in unit 1. The led groups, however, used more superordinates than the unled groups

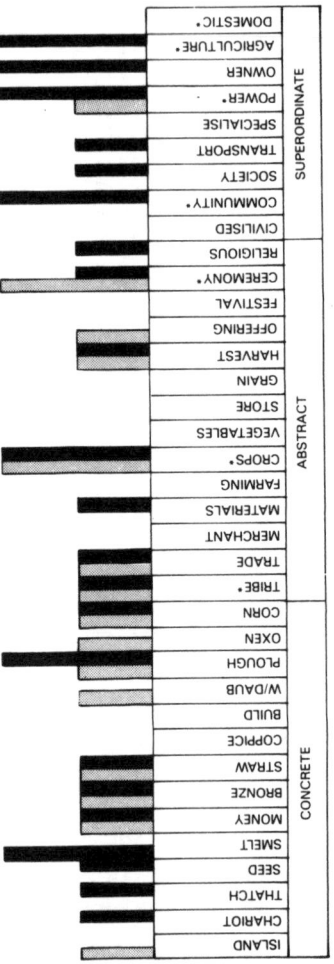

Note: * concepts learned in unit 1.

149

Figure 6.4: *Concepts taught in unit 1 or unit 2 which were used in written evidence tests in unit 4 by Exp 1, Exp 2 and control group children*

This bar chart shows how children in both experimental groups retained concepts learned in units 1 and 2 and applied them in their answers to unit 4. The control group used no abstract key concepts

▨ represents 1 concept used by Exp 1 group child
▨ represents 1 concept used by Exp 2 group child
▨ represents 1 concept used by control group child

	Concrete	*Abstract*	*Superordinate*
Exp 1	9	34	15
Exp 2	11	29	5
C	2	2	0

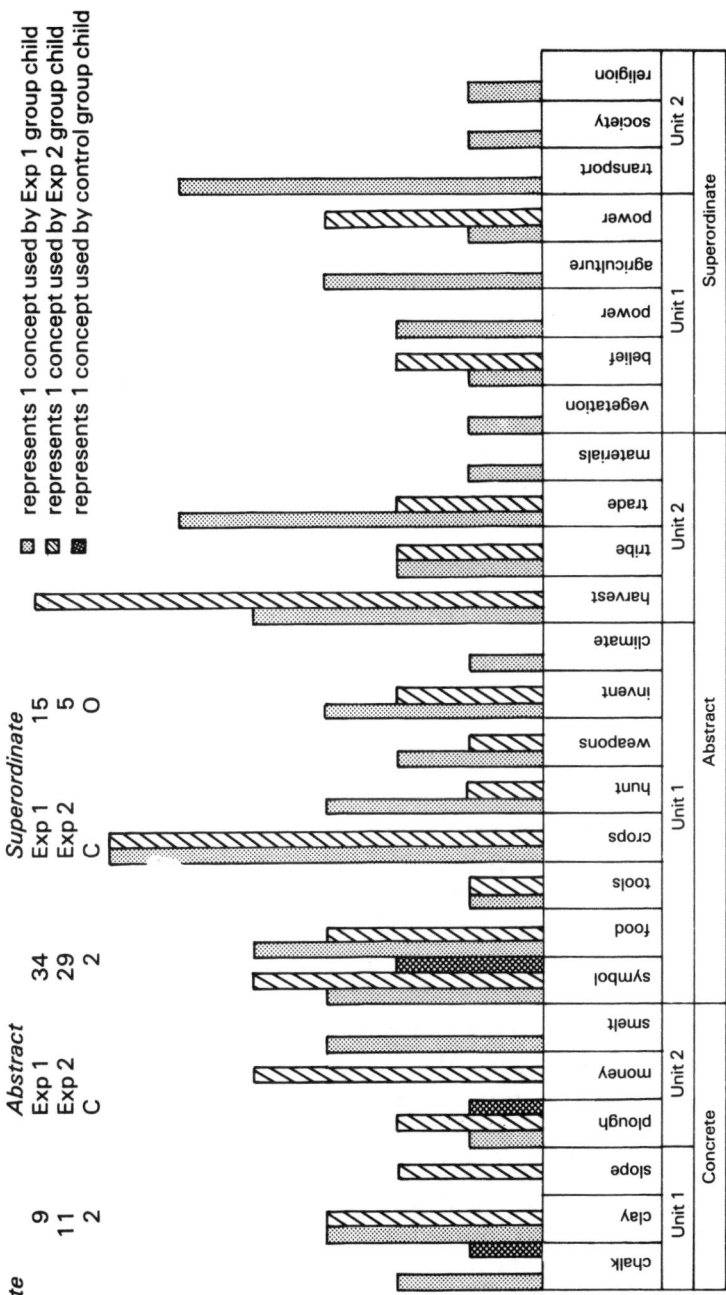

There are implications here for older students. It has often been assumed that artefacts and pictures are more appropriate for younger children who cannot read and write easily. However, if tangible sources are not easier to interpret, this strengthens the case for using a range of sources at any level of study.

Again, it is important to bear in mind that while the main effects shown in Figure 6.2 are statistically significant, there were variations in this pattern, influenced by particular examples of evidence, and by teaching strategies. In unit 4, the level main effect across the five kinds of evidence resulted from opposite trends across the experimental and control groups, although the span was only across one mark. It is likely that the control group found the Beowulf extract easier to interpret than the other evidence because they had more experience of 'comprehension exercises' but they had not learned how to interpret historical evidence.

Using learned concepts

The concepts which children had been taught in each unit as 'spellings' and which they had learned to use in discussing key evidence during class lessons the following week were used spontaneously by at least some of the children in both the written tests and the taped discussions. It was also encouraging that in unit 4, they were using vocabulary which they had learned in connection with previous units, transferring it to a new period and new material. Not surprisingly, the children in the control group who had not learned specific concepts only used those which were labelled in the evidence, and these were rarely abstract concepts. Figure 6.3 and Figure 6.4 show how children used concepts they had learned in previous units in both written and oral evidence tests.

Although no claim is made that the children totally understood the abstract concepts they used (e.g. vegetation, belief, power, agriculture, transport, society, religion), it seems that these concepts are becoming part of their own vocabulary.

It may be that the experimental groups were able to make a far greater range of valid suppositions about the evidence because they had a conceptual framework of both concrete and abstract concepts to which they could relate new pieces of evidence, even if the concepts themselves were not mentioned in their answers. Freedman and Loftus (1971) concluded that concepts play an important part in organising semantic memory. For example, in interpreting the written evidence in the Iron Age unit (see p. 144) many children make deductions concerned with trade, agriculture, metal production and social structure.

IW 'We know that Grece people traded with us . . . they must have had something to trade with.'

FF 'We know that gold, silver and iron are all exported across the see.'

NH 'They had corn and cattle . . . they could farm and so they had learned to live in one place . . . .'

MF guessed that 'since they had gold, silver and iron, they had miners' and he wondered how they mined and transported it because he had seen neither mining tools nor Iron Age boats in pictures.

Similarly, in interpreting the illuminated Saxon manuscript showing harvest, children in the experimental groups focused on ideas connected with agriculture, community, and communication. They discussed crops, farming methods and the cycle of the farming year.

RD 'The people seem to be cutting logs and transporting them – maybe to trade them – if they lived near a forest.'

They refer to the jobs people are doing and the relationship between them, and make various suggestions about the meaning of the writing.

It seems then that not only do children enjoy learning to use and spell 'hard words', but that learning key concepts gives them a reference point, or framework, to apply to new material, and that this helps to generate a range of new ideas about it.

Led and unled group discussion

The content of the discussion was similar in both the led and unled groups. It was concerned with how the evidence may have been used and what it may have meant to those who created it, although the children had not been asked at any point to consider these aspects. However, the groups differed in the way they expressed their ideas. The led groups tended to make general statements and seemed to assume that the teacher knew where the discussion was leading, whereas the unled groups paid more attention to physical description, and sometimes explained their ideas through valid stories and images, about brave warriors for example, who may be commemorated by a stone circle, or who may have hidden their treasure there and defended

Diagram 6.4: *A comparison of the content of the led and unled discussions about previously unseen evidence. Unit 4. The Saxons*

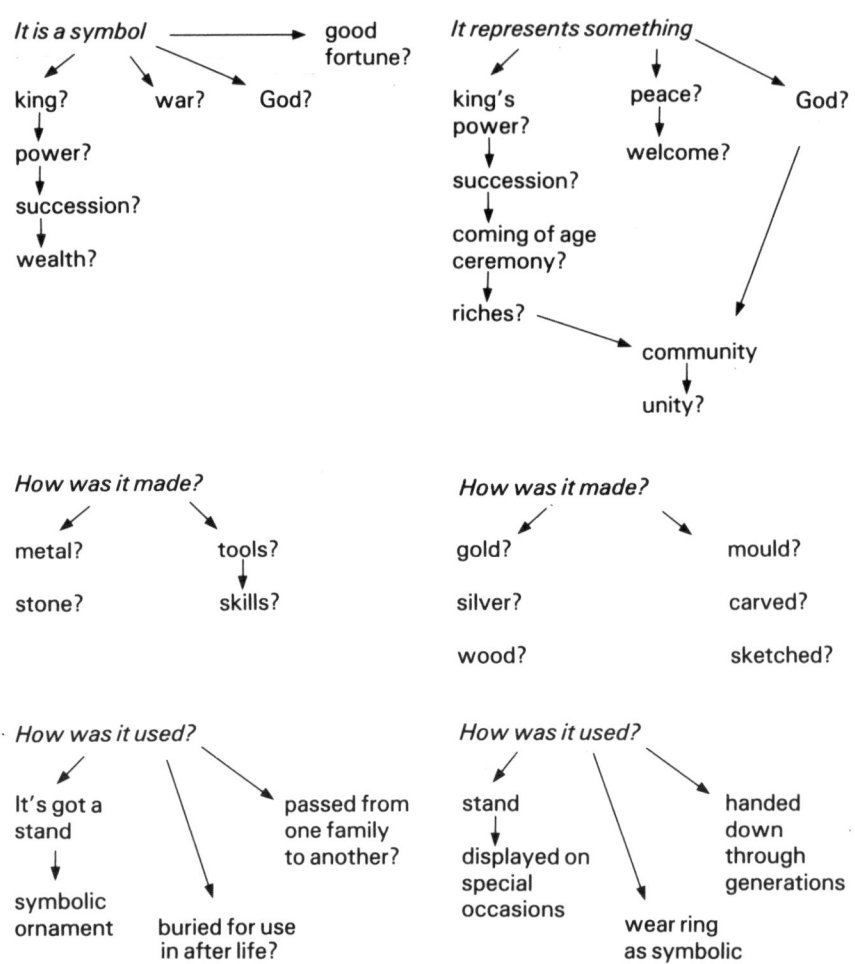

Led Discussion   *Unled Discussion*

Test 1. Artefact. The Sutton Hoo Sceptre

It is a symbol ⟶ good fortune?

king?   war?   God?

power?

succession?

wealth?

It represents something

king's power?   peace?   God?

succession?   welcome?

coming of age ceremony?

riches? → community

unity?

How was it made?

metal?   tools?

stone?   skills?

How was it made?

gold?   mould?

silver?   carved?

wood?   sketched?

How was it used?

It's got a stand   passed from one family to another?

symbolic ornament   buried for use in after life?

How was it used?

stand   handed down through generations

displayed on special occasions   wear ring as symbolic bracelet?

Diagram 6.4: *Cont*

| *Led Discussion* | *Unled Discussion* |

Test 2. Illuminated Picture of Harvest from Saxon Calendar

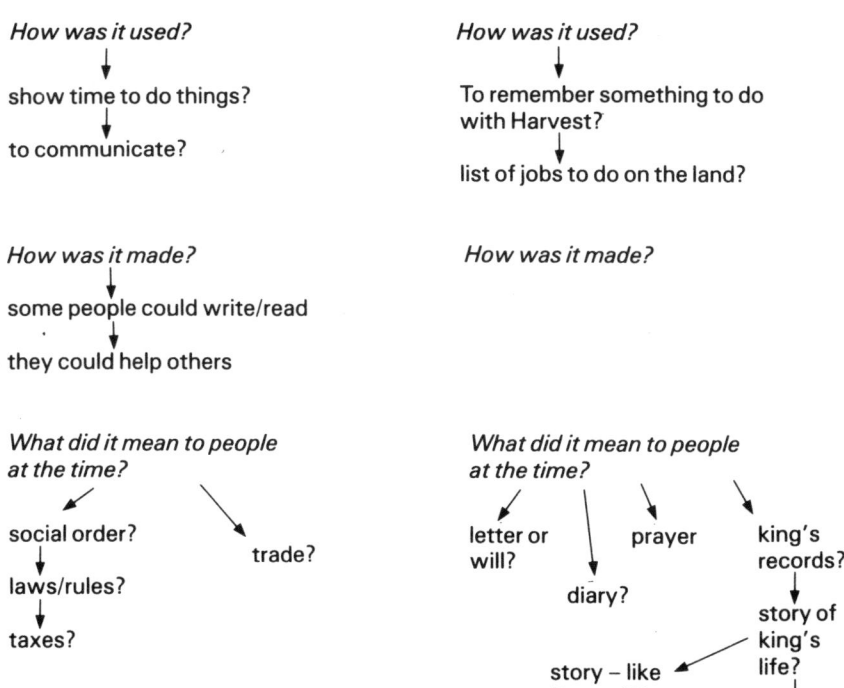

How was it used?

show time to do things?

to communicate?

How was it used?

To remember something to do with Harvest?

list of jobs to do on the land?

How was it made?

some people could write/read

they could help others

How was it made?

What did it mean to people at the time?

social order?

laws/rules?

taxes?

trade?

What did it mean to people at the time?

letter or will?

prayer

king's records?

diary?

story of king's life?

story – like Beowulf?

tax/rent?

Test 3. Diagram. Plan of Saxon Church at Cirencester

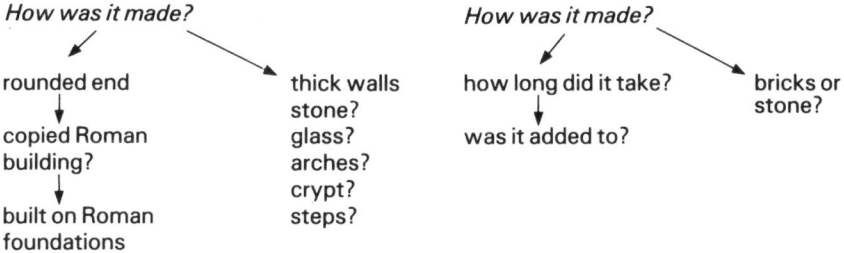

How was it made?

rounded end

copied Roman building?

built on Roman foundations

thick walls
stone?
glass?
arches?
crypt?
steps?

How was it made?

how long did it take?

was it added to?

bricks or stone?

Diagram 6.4: *Cont*

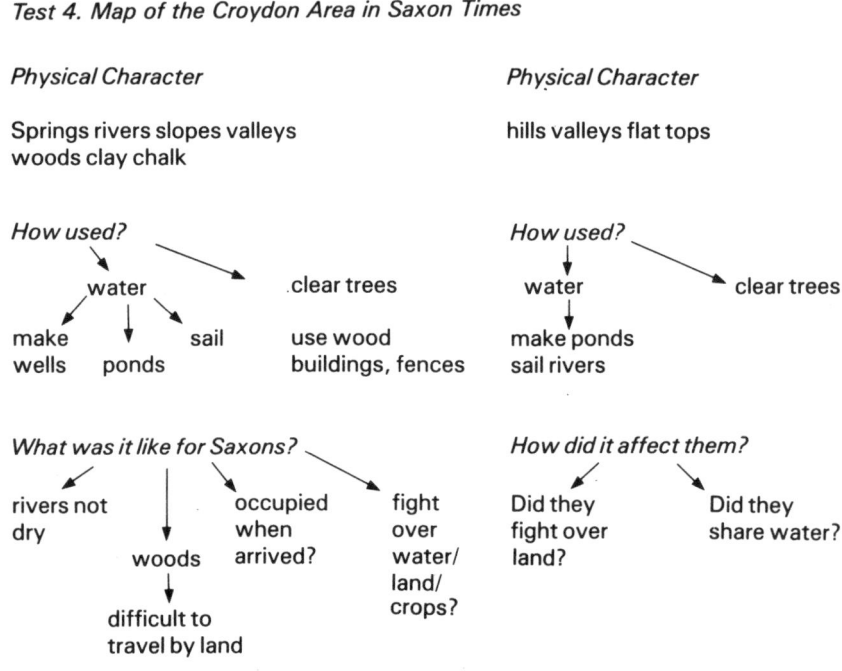

Led Discussion

How was it used?

crypt

store wine?
sick room?
meetings?
important people?

nave

what kind of service?
what beliefs?

Unled Discussion

How was it used?

aisles?   vicar?   services?
statues?
cross?   christenings?
holy water?   how often?
                       childrens'
            special   chapel?
            robes?   kneel?

Test 4. Map of the Croydon Area in Saxon Times

Physical Character

Springs rivers slopes valleys
woods clay chalk

Physical Character

hills valleys flat tops

How used?

water   clear trees

make   sail   use wood
wells ponds   buildings, fences

How used?

water   clear trees

make ponds
sail rivers

What was it like for Saxons?

rivers not   occupied   fight
dry   when   over
        woods   arrived?   water/
                              land/
    difficult to   crops?
    travel by land

How did it affect them?

Did they   Did they
fight over   share water?
land?

it. However, in both the led and unled groups, there was genuine argument. They both made some illogical points. In the unled groups, they were either ignored or corrected, with respect, by another child. In the led groups, it was usually the teacher who queried them. In both groups, the children developed each other's points and the quality of the discussion improved over the four units. There was an increase in the numbers of points made and in the number of sequential arguments, and a decrease in the number of illogical points. The structure of the discussions differed slightly in the led and unled groups. The led groups tended to explore all the possibilities suggested by one point, then move on to the next point whereas the unled groups usually followed up a point with one further argument, then made a fresh point. Sometimes, they back-tracked, and ideas were less systematically explored.

It seems then that both led and unled discussions have a place in helping children to interpret evidence. If children have learned the thinking patterns required, discussion in small groups without the teacher may sometimes be more valuable than teacher-led discussion; children are more able to explain their ideas in their own way, to defend them and so to make them their own. This has implications for classroom organisation and for the value of group work not directly led by the teacher.

Teaching strategies

Visits

The children were able to transfer information learned on visiting a site to new evidence. For example, on the visit to Farthing Down, they had been asked how, if they had lived there in Neolithic times, they could have made a dry, warm, comfortable shelter, what they could have eaten, where they might have found water, how they might have made tools, weapons and pots. When given a map of another similar area of the North Downs they were able to apply these points to the new map and make a range of deductions and suggestions in their written answers. Table 6.2 shows the information children had discussed on their visit to Farthing Down on the left. This visit stimulated their deductions about the map of a similar but unknown area which are given on the right.

The scores were surprisingly high for such abstract evidence; this seems to be because the visit enabled the children to relate real

Table 6.2: *Examples of written answers, showing how visit to Farthing Down helped children to interpret the map*

Evidence discussed on visit to Farthing Down	Children's use of this evidence applied to the test map (Exp Group A) Written Evidence
Geology: Top of Down is chalk with flints. Sparse vegetation and well-drained.	CL Qu 1. They had a lot of chalk. They could build huts on it because it's flat. They would not build a hut at the bottom of the hill because the water would not run away. (Score level 8) AM Qu 2. They could have camped on the slopes because when it rained the rain would run down the slope. If people lived on a slope, their camp would not be flooded and their huts would not get destroyed. (Score level 7) CL Qu 3. I would like to know what flint implements were used for because they already had hand tools for killing animals. (Score level 6)
Clay soil – sticky – heavy	HC It has got a lot of clay on the surfis . . . it must of been soggy. It must of been very wet. (Score level 7) IW Qu 2. I can guess that they made things . . . they would use clay to built pots. We can also guess that there is chalk . . . there is flint. (Score level 8) HC Qu 2. There might have been a lot of wetness . . . it could of been cold. There might of been stone age people living there . . . they might of been living on the chalk bits.
In valley bottom there is marsh and a stream	ML Qu 2. They might have routes to the rivers . . . they would have an easy way to go. They used pots to get water . . . they can get water in time. (Score level 8)
Hachures show slopes	KM Qu 1. We know that Hachures mean steep slopes . . . the hachures on the map mean there are shallow and steep slopes. (Score level 7)
Vegetation (+Geology) grass on top yew and oak on clay slopes	JW Qu 2. I can guess what kind of trees grew there . . . I think oak and fir trees grew there. There were big chalk and clay areas where they could make pots. They could of lived near the clay area so they wouldn't have to walk far. (Score level 8)

Table 6.2: *Cont*

Evidence discussed on visit to Farthing Down	Children's use of this evidence applied to the test map (Exp Group A) Written Evidence
	CL Qu 2. We can guess which plants they used for medicine . . . some people knew which plants cure illnesses. We can also guess which plants and leaves they used for a bed . . . they would choose the best things to make it. So they would select things to use. (Score level 7)
Animals	ES Qu 3. I would like to know if animals lived there when Stone Age lived because I want to see if they ate small animals.

Examples. Experimental Group 2. Unit 1. Test 4. Showing use of visit in interpreting map

Geology: chalk/flint, clay, slope, wind, river	PC (level 8) Qu 1. They found that chalk sucks the water through it . . . we know it was dry. They lived in places like Farthing Down.
	DF (level 9) Qu 2. They lived near to chalk and clay areas . . . they didn't have to go far to get flints. They lived near slopes . . . they were in a place with not many trees. They knew exactly where to live.
	JG (level 8) Qu 2. I guess they could have shelter from the cliffs . . . they would be safe. They would have water . . . they could have land for farming on the chalk soil.
	FB (level 8) Qu 2. They probably went fishing in the river . . . they probably had quite a lot of fish. They probably had to wash in the river . . . they probably didn't wash much!
	JG (level 8) Qu 1. Neolithic people must have been in the area . . . they had camps there. Trees might be in great numbers on the clay soil . . . they had shelter.
Vegetation	MF (level 7) Qu 3. Why they chose that place. What animals lived there, because I'd like to know what they ate.
	RF (level 7) Qu 2. I can guess there must have been a lot of woods . . . I can guess there must have been lots of
Animals	animals nearby. I know there must have been a lot of food nearby.

158

Figure 6.5: *How children were able to transfer their discussion of Iron Age field patterns seen on a visit to Farthing Down to a previously unseen map of field systems on Butser Hill, Hants.*

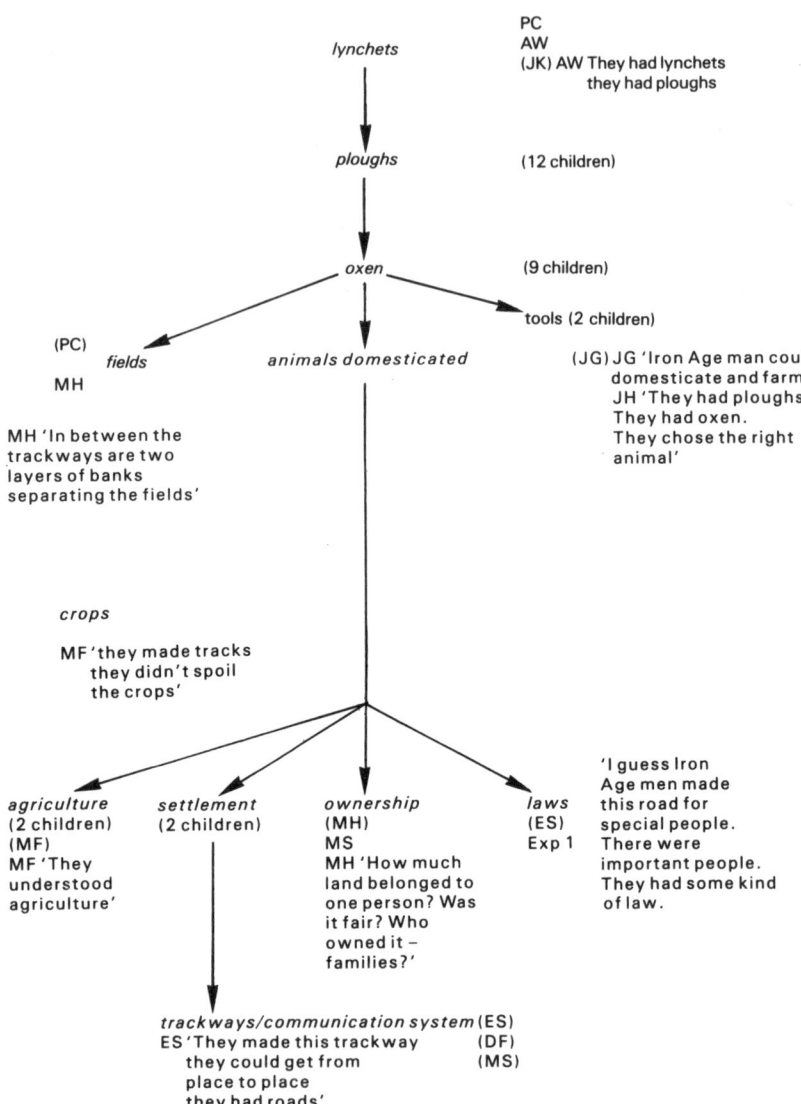

experiences and images to the map. As AW wrote in his conclusion 'This is the *best* evidence game'!

Similarly, in the Iron Age unit, they had again visited Farthing Down to trace the lynchets, the soil banks formed by turning the plough, which indicate Iron Age field patterns. Figure 6.5 shows how

Table 6.3:

Butser Map	Farthing Down Visit	Class Discussion	Own Ideas
PC There are bumps. We know where the fields were	They could use machinery like a plough. They farmed. They grew crops.	There was probably a settlement there. They probably grew *vegetables* (re: evidence of beans, vetch, crop rotation)	If they thought the horse was a god or something why did they not use it? (in farming)
JG They had ploughs	They understood how to grow crops. They could farm and domesticate	There might be *tools* or there might be bones of oxen still there. (re: evidence of bones found, and tools, at Glastonbury) (re: oxen bones similar to modern Dexter)	A cart could carry crops from the field. How long did it take to make (invent?) a cart? If there are bones there, archaeologists could make up an oxen like they make dinosaurs in Natural History Museum
RF I know for certain this map gives us clues. I know some people can find these ditches (i.e I know they exist and what they look like)	I guess they had patterns in soil and chalk (i.e I know soil or chalk is thin – viz the Uffington Horse)	I guess they had *lambs* (re: sheep probably Soay, as at Butser) or as JK said' sheep would give wool and meat and keep the grass down	
MS They had fields. They must have had a plough	I guess the tracks were for taking the plough across	They might grow things like peas and beans (re: Butser evidence)	I guess the tracks were made of wood. There must have been timber to make them from. I would like to know what transport they had, and we would know what skills they had

Table 6.3: *Cont*

Butser Map	Farthing Down Visit	Class Discussion	Own Ideas
SK They had roads	They could take the oxen across to another field because if the plough went over the corn it would crush it up and it would not grow again	I think they had a field of *herbs* (re: discussion of flavouring and preserving)	They could eat them and (use them to) make other foods
MH In between the two trackways are two layers of banks separating the fields	They must transport the plough through gaps in the banks	The blank bits might be for *settlements* (re: post hole evidence)	Maybe the owners might live there. Maybe ownership separated by trackways. I would like to know how much land belonged to one person; if they had the same amount and if they lived in families next to each other

they were able to transfer discussion of these to the Iron Age map fields at Butser, on the South Downs.

At the end of unit 2 the children were given a previously unseen map of Iron Age fields on Butser Hill in Hampshire. In their written answers, experimental group 2 developed between them many of the arguments inherent in this evidence, which showed lynchets and trackways.

Table 6.3 analyses how children in the written answers related the new evidence about Butser to their visit to Farthing Down, and also to their class discussion on Iron Age farming, and finally to their own ideas. This shows how they were able to transfer the experience of the visit and following class discussion to new evidence, and, in doing so, also to form their own valid suggestions and questions.

The visits probably also helped them to discuss the plans of a stone circle, an Iron Age hut, and a Saxon church, although they had not visited similar sites, because they had considered geology, vegetation and relief, and the effects of these on a settlement in each period.

The stimulus of the 'further afield' visit to Grimes Graves and the British Museum probably helped the experimental groups to make a greater range of suppositions than the control group about artefacts, about the Stone-Age axe-heads, for example, and the Waterloo Helmet.

Language: discussion, concepts and language as an objective tool

Discussion

Class lessons were based on discussion of selected evidence, using learned concepts. Each unit consisted of four such lessons taught over consecutive weeks. One of the four lessons was based on the local visit to an area of settlement, and one focused on ideas and beliefs.

This study endorsed the importance of learning through open-ended discussion, in which children learn the thinking processes of history. They learn that many suggestions are possible, and remain uncertain, and that arguments must be supported and can be contested. This is how criteria for validity become understood. It seems likely that this is the most important factor in the difference between the control group and experimental groups' responses. Firstly, the experimental groups achieved both a higher level of inferential reasoning, and a wider range of valid suppositions. Secondly, the control and experimental groups used the factual information they had in different ways. They were not required to rehearse it in their answers but nevertheless, it underpinned their answers. The control group, however, tended to repeat information given, which was only loosely related to the evidence, and when they went beyond it, they often revealed misconceptions. The experimental groups were more likely to test given knowledge against the evidence. Their suggestions, for example, about the Anglo-Saxon sceptre were dependent on their knowledge of Anglo-Saxon kings and kingdoms, laws and succession.

It seems, then, that discussion is important in the development of historical understanding. However the discussion must be based on selected key evidence. Children need key factual information, but if they learn it through discussion, they do not simply repeat it, but they both retain the information and are able to transfer the pattern of discursive thinking to new evidence.

Concepts

The importance of teaching and using selected concepts of different levels of abstraction to interpret key evidence has already been discussed (p. 150). It was seen that children were able to use abstract, learned concepts as an organising framework against which to test new evidence, even when they did not mention the concept itself. This helped them in discussing the Sutton Hoo sceptre to talk about the king, ceremonies, symbols and laws; Beowulf deductions involved power, vengeance, courage and beliefs. Learned concepts helped children to make a greater range of valid suggestions about evidence, to develop arguments, and so to make suggestions about different attitudes, behaviour and beliefs.

Language as an objective tool

The experimental groups had also discussed the nature of language as a tool for communication. They were able to talk about the relationship between the written and spoken word, the symbolism of language and to suppose how language originated and changed. A child could say of the Stone Age petroglyphics, for instance, 'They made signs for communicating; they had things to draw with; they needed people.' Or 'They wrote strange writing . . . they had different words from today. This writing is found in Italy . . . it could have been found in other places . . .'. One child wrote, 'They had to teach each other how to speak . . . they had to co-operate in making writing.'

Another guessed that in different countries they had different signs ... if someone went to a different country, he would not understand. It took a long time to carve the signs ... they would not move from place to place.

In considering the Strabo excerpt in unit 2, JG wondered 'how long after the Romans the Iron Age wrote.' AW observed that 'they had different language over different times. They did not have the same language everywhere ... I would like to know how they made their languages up ...'.

In unit 4, JG wondered, 'if the Saxons learned writing from the Romans,' but AW and DS guessed it was learned through the monks. 'I guess the monks wrote it. It would be in Latin.' 'Monks were taut to read and rit in neat ritting ....' SH guessed that since they could write and were good at drawing, 'they probably had lituriture.' In interpreting the extract from Beowulf, children considered the significance of the language. 'I would like to know what Gaet means.' 'I would like to know why Grendel was called Grendel. It sounds strange. Is Grendel a Latin name or an English name?' 'I think that 'gable roof' is the bit just below the top of the house.' They also tried to explore the significance of writing in Saxon times. 'It is a Saxon poem. Therefore they had forms of writing. Beowulf was made up. Therefore it would be a folk tale or a legend ....'

Acceleration

The study suggested that if children are taught consistently, applying the same teaching strategies to new material, they learn patterns of thinking which can be transferred, and the quality of their thinking improves. In unit 4, the experimental groups achieved higher levels of deductive argument than in previous units, and used more abstract concepts. It seems then that it is important for children to learn patterns of thinking, and for teachers to be clear what these should be. In unit 4, although the means for all three groups were higher than in the first two units, the means for the experimental groups were much higher than the control group mean (Figure 6.6).

The integrated curriculum

The study did not aim to prove the benefits of learning history through an integrated curriculum. However, the links between responses to the history tests and other areas of the curriculum can be traced. From the

Figure 6.6: *Graph showing means of evidence test scores for control and experimental groups for units 1, 2 and 4*

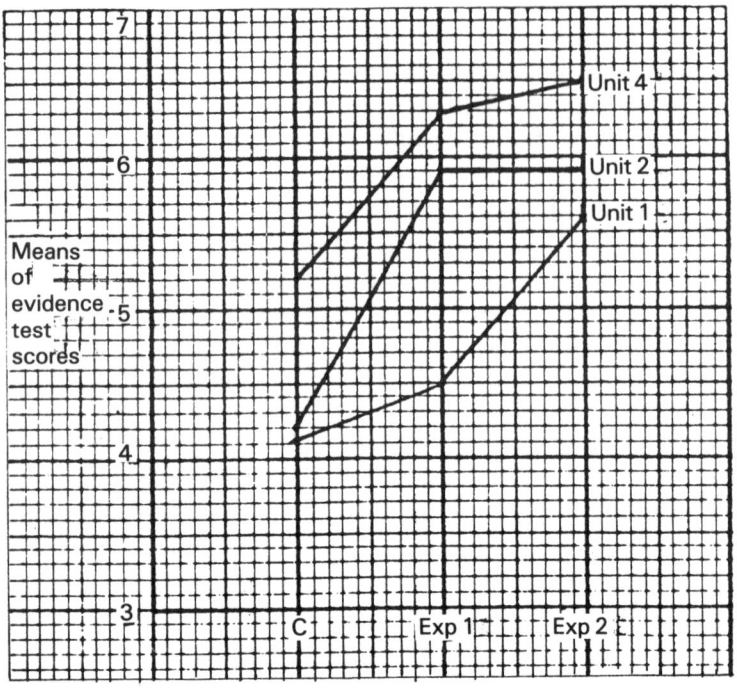

science components, the children seem to have learned both to question and respect the technology of other societies.

They discuss how things were made and used. For example, the discussion of the Waterloo Helmet reflects their knowledge of iron smelting learned in the Iron Age unit. Their experience of historical fiction (*The Changeling*, R. Sutcliffe; *The Dream Time and The Bronze Sword*, H. Treece) may well have helped children to recognise the difference between fact and imagination. There are many examples of children transferring their knowledge of geology, vegetation and relief to maps of other areas; geography probably also influenced their references to trade, transport, and migration of peoples. Art taught the experimental groups careful observation through drawing (slides of cave paintings, Iron Age artefacts in the British Museum, or Anglo-Saxon pottery). It also seems to have taught them both an interest in the techniques and materials used in the past, and an understanding and respect for different interpretations. SH guesses that 'Stone Age people may have kept their oxides in pots and used their hands to paint.' The experimental groups suggest why the Uffington Horse may be unrealistic. DS NVR 88 (Exp 1. Qu 1 (7)) owns a horse and brings her own keen interest to bear, in spite of difficulties with spelling!

> I kown that they had Horse Because it is a piter of one. They must of copid the Bones of the Horse And the shape of the Horse And it must of bein bukin because of its back legs and the sape of it . . .

MH NVR 135 (Exp 2. Qu 1 (9))

> Two of the legs do not join up to the body. Therefore I think that is a special 3D effect. It has whiskers on a kind of chin. Therefore either they have not observed well, or their horse has whiskers.

The dimension of religious education involved the discussion of the symbolism of light and dark in cave-painting and in other cultures, the needs and fears of Iron Age people, the nature of Roman Gods, the teachings of early Celtic and Roman missionaries. It may be that this helped children to consider reasons for beliefs and rituals in their own and other societies. The mathematics component may have encouraged deductions involving estimates. ('It might take 1000 people to fill the church. The population must have been big.') They consider shape. One child says of the circle, 'They had another shape in maths,' and the Uffington Horse has a 'special 3D effect'. The Iron Age fields are 'square or rectangular'.

An integrated project with a clear history focus seems the most economical way, in a crowded curriculum, to allow children to become steeped in a period. It also demonstrates that history involves the history of thought in all disciplines and in all aspects of society, and can, in turn, give a purpose to experiment in science and to calculations in mathematics.

Ways in which teachers can evaluate and develop the National Curriculum in the light of experience and good practice

This research indicates some of the problems involved in assessing patterns in the development of children's thinking in history. However, the study was undertaken as an integral part of class teaching, and refined the thinking of the teacher and the quality of her teaching in the process, so that it suggests that action research by practising teachers is both possible and desirable, and should therefore be supported and encouraged.

It is not necessary for such detailed analysis to be carried out all the time, or by all teachers; the purpose of the study described was to indicate broad patterns of development, and the relationship between different aspects of historical thinking which could form a basis for planning and for on-going assessment by teachers. It is essential that the broad brushstrokes with which the National Curriculum aims to paint a map of the past is also balanced by detailed and carefully focused discussion of key evidence. Young children cannot grasp a holistic view of complex social structures; they do not understand the workings of adult minds, addressing difficult political and religious issues. They need some indication of the causes of the English Civil War, but are not interested in detailed, received, watered-down interpretations by historians. It seems likely that the need to list and memorise 'causes and effects' killed school history for many people and there is a danger that too much emphasis on content will reintroduce this approach.

Experience suggests that children are interested in detail, and in problem-solving in which they can be validly and genuinely engaged: how true do you think Lucy Hutchinson's account of the Siege of Nottingham is? What do the portraits of Charles I and of Cromwell tell us about them? What did sailors on the Armada ships eat? What did the sailors on the Mary Rose do? Who lived in my home before I did?

Therefore, the curriculum must be taught in an economical way if it is not to be overloaded. Planning must be carefully focused to centre on real problem-solving in each curriculum area, and in a range of contexts. Planning, activities and evaluation must form a related sequence so that assessment is an integral part of all the work children do and of the constant interaction between teacher and child. Work planned in history must reflect the thinking processes of history, and allow for a range of differentiated outcomes. It should also involve learning history through the rich variety of activities on which good primary practice is based:

- information technology (simulations, word-processing and data-handling);
- art (drawing, printing, painting, embroidery, model-making);
- science and technology (cooking, spinning, weaving, grinding seeds, building and testing structures, using tools, moving loads, using a range of materials);
- language for different audiences (transactional and expressive writing, reading, discussion, role-play, making video and audio tapes).

Assessment may be based on activities over different time-spans, a morning, a week, half a term. It may involve individuals, or groups. Activities may be chosen by the children or the teacher. They may involve parents and family visits, as well as school visits. They should deal with a variety of evidence, artefacts, pictures, diagrams, maps, writing. Assessment in history will inevitably be through language. This may be written, as labels explaining a display, as archeologists' reports, or as accounts, but more precise assessment and higher levels of thinking will almost certainly emerge through finding quick ways of recording group discussions, either in the classroom, or through analysing tapes. The research described in this chapter suggests ways in which spoken language may be assessed in history.

Assessment is important for children and for parents. The SEAC History Committee recommended that the Statements of Attainment should be brief so that children could be involved in recording their own progress and parents could help to develop their children's historical understanding, both by being able to talk to them about their work in school, and possibly to extend it, through accompanying school visits, making private visits or collecting resources. If parents are to value and support history, an aspect of education which they often regard as less important than the 'three Rs', they need to understand what is being taught, how and why; what the children are being asked to achieve and what the next stage is. Parents have usually been confident that they understand what constitutes progress in the 'basic skills' but not in history, and teachers have been less than articulate in remedying this. Consequently, history has been undervalued; it has been seen as interesting, but not central to education. For this reason, one school always begins a term by inviting parents to a meeting at which work planned is explained: what the children will be doing, how, and why.

A mother became sufficiently interested to watch a television programme about excavations at a Celtic hill fort which she talked about over breakfast the following morning with her eight-year-old son. 'But Mum,' he asked, 'what is the *evidence* for that?' One child, after a school visit to Canterbury Cathedral, took her grandparents on an informed investigation of their local cathedral in Norwich. (Another child, less well-supported by her family, read a lengthy and impressive poem about Beowulf to the milkman!)

Children also need to be explicitly aware of what they are learning to do, why it is important, and what the next step may be. It is therefore helpful to devise methods for self-assessment by children, or for collaborative evaluation between children and teacher.

Attempts to interpret the Statements of Attainment form a useful agenda for discussion with colleagues. This could be a framework for providing a bank of information and for further research, either as small-scale studies by groups of teachers which could be published in such journals as *Teaching History*, or as contributions to research on a national scale. Exhibitions in teachers' centres may reflect and stimulate collaborative work. It would be interesting to know, for instance, whether historical sources can be categorised according to 'levels of difficulty', and, if so, what constitutes these levels. The problem is compounded because the complexities of interpretation and of evidence interact; these can be complex interpretations of simple evidence and vice-versa. It should be possible to find similar but different evidence and test children of the same age on the same periods using the same teaching strategies and achieve similar results. However, the problem of familiarity would remain. Donaldson (1978) showed that children reason more competently about material that is familiar. It would be interesting to see if similar evidence could be found for early periods and recent periods (about which there is more known information, and the differences between past and present may be more subtle), to find out whether children make similar numbers of valid suppositions about evidence for different periods. A cross-sectional study would be interesting over a wide age-range using the same questions but increasingly complex evidence (maybe one piece of evidence, then several pieces of evidence, then conflicting evidence, and finally, evidence showing bias and representing other viewpoints). Alternatively, children could be given the same evidence, but increasingly complex questions. Longitudinal studies could provide a greater understanding of sequences and patterns of development in relation to different teaching strategies. Very young children's understanding of concepts of time would be very interesting to investigate more fully.

Although there are many questions still unanswered, the National Curriculum is the first attempt to ensure that all children learn about the past through active involvement in the problems of understanding time and change, and of interpreting different kinds of evidence, in a progressive way. The establishment of such an approach to history in the primary curriculum constitutes an advance in the education of young children because it synthesises two previously antithetical assumptions about early learning. It has long been appreciated that effective learning takes place, through interaction with the physical environment and with other people's responses to it.

For this very reason, there has been emphasis on 'concrete operations', on offering to young children an education based on direct physical and sensory experiences. Consequently, they were not thought capable of genuine historical problem-solving. Experience strongly suggests that this is not so, that children particularly enjoy history-focused topics, and both they and non-specialist teachers derive great pleasure from grappling with real, if simple, historical problems, from internalising the material, making it their own, and so feeling that they are acquiring control over their own thinking. It will be teachers' ability to plan work which focuses on different aspects of historical problem-solving as an on-going part of the process of learning which will raise the quality and the significance of primary school history. Certainly, history fulfils the criteria of Bruner (1963, p. 52) for any subject taught in a primary school, that when fully developed, it is worth an adult's knowing, and having known it as a child, makes a person a better adult.

If history is to be established as an essential aspect of a broad primary curriculum, it will be through the conviction, enthusiasm, and efforts of class teachers. They are the practitioners. They must provide evidence for the ways in which, and the extent to which, the National Curriculum for history can work. It is important that they have the confidence to recognise and assume this challenge.

> It is a living model . . . (which) will undoubtedly evolve as the demands of education evolve . . . I strongly recognise the importance of teachers themselves being involved in this process . . . '
>
> (Address by Rt. Hon. John McGregor,
> Proceedings of Assistant Masters and
> Mistresses Association, 1990, p. 11)

References

AMMA (1990) Proceedings of the Assistant Masters and Mistresses Association Address by Rt. Honourable John McGregor.

Ashby, R. and Lee, P.J. (1987) 'Children's Concepts of Empathy and Understanding in History', in C. Portal (ed.) *The History Curriculum for Teachers*. Lewes: Falmer Press.

Ausubel, D.P. (1963) *The Psychology of Meaningful Verbal Learning*. Gruse.

Ausubel, D.P. (1968) *Educational Psychology. A Cognitive View*. London: Holt, Rinehart and Winston.

Barnes, D. and Todd, F. (1977) *Communication and Learning in Small Groups*. London: Routledge and Kegan Paul.

Beard, R.M. (1960) 'The Nature and Development of Concepts', in *Educational Review* 13, No. 1, pp.12–26.

Beattie, A. (1987) *History in Peril: May Parents Preserve It*. London: Centre for Policy Studies.

Beddoe, D. (1983) *Discovering Women's History*. London: Pandora.

Bernot, L. and Blancard, R. (1953) *Nouville, un Village Francis*. Paris: Institut d'Ethnologie.

Bersu, G. (1940) *Excavations at Little Woodbury* 6, pp.30–111.

Biott, C. (1984) Getting on Without the Teacher. Primary School Pupils in Co-operative Groups. Collaborative Research Paper 1. Sunderland Polytechnic. Schools Council Programme Two.

Blakeway, S.E. (1983) 'Some Aspects of the Historical Understanding of Children aged 7 to 11'. Unpub. MA Dissertation. London University Institute of Education.

Blyth, A. (1990) *Making the Grade for Primary Humanities*. Milton Keynes: Open University Press.

Blyth, J.E. (1982) *History in Primary Schools*. McGraw Hill. Open University Press (2nd edn., 1989).

Blyth, J.E. (1988) *History 5–9*. London: Hodder and Stoughton.

Booth, M.B. (1969) *History Betrayed*. London: Longmans, Green and Co.

Booth, M. (1979) 'A Longitudinal Study of the Cognitive Skills, Concepts and Attitudes of Adolescents Studying a Modern World History Syllabus, and an Analysis of their Historical Thinking'. Unpub. PhD Thesis. University of Reading.

Borke, H. (1978) 'Piaget's View of Social Interaction and the Theoretical Construct of Empathy', in L. E. Siegal and C. J. Brainerd (eds.) *Alternatives to Piaget*. London: Academic Press.

Boulding, E. (1976) *Handbook of International Data on Women*. Beverley Hills Sage.

Boulding, E. (1977) *Women in the Twentieth Century World*. New York: Sage.

Boulding, G. E. (1981) *The Underside of History*. Westview.

Bruner, J. S. (1963) *The Process of Education*. New York: Vintage Books.

Bruner, J. S. (1966) *Towards a Theory of Instruction*. The Belknap Press of Harvard U.P. (7th Ed, 1975).

Butterworth, G. and Light, P. (1982) (eds.) *Social Cognition – Studies in the Development of Understanding*. Brighton: Harvester Press.

Clarke, R. R. (1960) *East Anglia*.

Collingwood, R. G. (1939) *An Autobiography* (pbk, 1970). London: Oxford University Press.

Coltham, J. (1960) 'Junior School Children's Understanding of Historical Terms'. Unpub. PhD Thesis. University of Manchester.

Cooper, H. J. (1991) 'Young Children's Thinking in History'. Unpub. PhD Thesis. London University Institute of Education.

Cowie, E. E. (1985) *History and the Slow Learning Child*. Teaching History Series. H.A. No. 41.

Cox, M. V. (1986) *The Development of Cognition and Language*. Brighton: Harvester Press.

Crowther, E. (1982) 'Understanding of the Concept of Change among Children and Young Adolescents'. *Educational Review* 34, 3, pp.279–84.

Croydon and Stockport Workhouse. Community Information Resource Project (1989) Davidson Professional Centre. Croydon.

Da Silva, W. A. (1969) 'Concept Formation in History through Conceptual Clues'. Unpub. PhD Thesis. University of Birmingham.

Davis, J. (1986) *Artefacts in the Primary School*. Teaching History Series. No. 45, pp.6–8. The Historical Association.

DES (1978) 'Primary Education in England and Wales'. Survey by Her Majesty's Inspectors of Schools. London: HMSO.

DES (1982) *Education 5–9*. London: HMSO.

DES (1983) *9–13 Middle Schools: An Illustrative Survey*. London: HMSO.

DES (1986) *History in Primary and Secondary Schools*. London: HMSO.

DES (1989) *The Teaching and Learning of History and Geography*. London: HMSO.

DES (1991) *Inspection of Humanities Courses in Years 5–9 in 26 Schools*. London: HMSO.

DES (1991a) *History in the National Curriculum*. London: HMSO.

Dickinson, A. K. and Lee, P. J. (1978) (eds) *History Teaching and Historical Understanding*. London: Heinemann.

Doise, W., Mugny, C. and Perret Clermont, A. N. (1975) 'Social Interaction and the Development of Cognitive Operations', in *European Journal of Social Psychology* 5, pp.367–83.

Doise, W. (1978) *Groups and Individuals: Explanations in Social Psychology*. Cambridge: Cambridge University Press.

Doise, W. and Mugny, G. (1979) 'Individual and Collective Conflicts of Centrations in Cognitive Development', in *European Journal of Social Psychology* 9, pp.105–9.

Donaldson, M. (1978) *Children's Minds*. London: Fontana.

Elton, G. R. (1970) 'What Sort of History Should we Teach?', in M. Ballard (ed.) *New Movements in the Study and Teaching of History*. Temple Smith.

Erikson, E. H. (1965) *Childhood and Society*. Harmondsworth: Penguin.

Famous Sailors (1970) Macdonald.

Flavell, J. H. (1985) *Cognitive Development* (2nd Edn). London and New York: Prentice Hall.

Freedman, J. L. and Loftus, E. F. (1971) 'Retrieval of Words from Long-Term Memory', in *Journal of Verbal Learning and Verbal Behaviour*, 10, pp.107–15.

Fryer, P. (1984) *Staying Power*. London: Pluto Press.

Fryer, P. (1989) *Black People in the British Empire – An Introduction*. London: Pluto Press.

Furth, H. G. (1980) The World of Grown Ups. New York: Elsevier.

Gagné, R. M. (1977) *The Conditions of Learning*. Rinehart and Winston.

Galton, M., Simon, B. and Croll, C. (1980) *Inside the Primary Classroom*. London: Routledge and Kegan Paul.

Garfield, L. and Blishen, E. (1970) *The God Beneath the Sea*. London: Longman.

Getzels, J. W. and Jackson, P. W. (1962) *Creativity and Intelligence: Explorations with Students*. London and New York: Wiley.

Gittings, C. (1991) 'Portraits as Historical Evidence in the Primary School', in *Primary History Today*. Historical Association.

Goldstein, A. P. and Michels, G. Y. (1985) *Empathy: Developmental Training and Consequences*. Hillsdale N.J.: Lawrence Erlbaum Associates.

Guilford, J. P. (1959) 'Traits of Creativity' in H. H. Anderson (ed.) *Creativity and Its Cultivation*, pp.142–61, Harper.

Haddon, F. A. and Lytton, H. (1968) 'Teaching Approach and the Development of Divergent Thinking Abilities in Primary Schools', in *British Journal of Educational Psychology*, Vol. 38, pp.171–80.

Hallam, R. N. (1975) 'A Study of the Effect of Teaching Method on the Growth of Logical Thought, with Special Reference to the Teaching of History using Criteria from Piaget's Theory of Cognitive Development'. Unpub. PhD Thesis. University of Leeds.

Hamlyn, D. (1982) 'What Exactly is Social about the Origins of Understanding?' in G. Butterworth and P. Light (eds.) *Social Cognition: Studies in the Development of Understanding*.

Harding, D. W. (1974) *The Iron Age in Lowland Britain*. London: Routledge and Kegan Paul.

Hill, C. (1980) *The World Turned Upside Down: Radical Ideas during the English Revolution*. Harmondsworth: Penguin.

Historical Association (1987) 'History in the Core Curriculum'.

HMI Wales (1989) *History in the Primary Schools of Wales*. Welsh Office.

Hodgkinson, K. (1986) 'How Artefacts can Stimulate Historical Thinking in Young Children'. *Education* 3–13, Vol. 14, No. 2.

174

Isaacs, S. (1948) *Intellectual Growth in Young Children*. London: Routledge and Kegan Paul.

Jahoda, G. (1963) 'Children's Concept of Time and History', in *Educational Review* 95.

Jones, R. M. (1968) *Fantasy and Feeling in Education*. London: London University Press.

Kitson Clarke, G. (1967) *The Critical Historian*. London: Heinemann.

Klausmeier, H. J. and Allen, P. S. (1978) *Cognitive Development of Children and Youth. A Longitudinal Study*. London: Academic Press.

Klausmeier, H. J. *et al.* (1979) *Cognitive Learning and Development*. Ballinger.

Knight, P. (1989a) 'Children's Understanding of People in the Past'. Unpub. PhD Thesis. University of Lancaster.

Knight, P. (1989b) 'Empathy: Concept, Confusion and Consequences in a National Curriculum', in *Oxford Review of Education* Vol. 15.

Knight, P. (1989c) 'A Study of Children's Understanding of People in the Past', in *Educational Review* Vol. 41, No. 3.

Lawton, D. (1975) *Class, Culture and the Curriculum*. London: Routledge and Kegan Paul.

Leach, E. (1973) 'Some Anthropological Observations on Number, Time and Common Sense', in G. A. Howson (ed.) *Developments in Mathematical Education*. Cambridge: Cambridge University Press.

Lello, J. (1980) 'The Concept of Time, the Teaching of History and School Organisation', in *History Teacher*. Vol. 13, No. 3.

Light, P. (1983) in S. Meadows (ed.) *Developing Thinking Approaches to Children's Cognitive Development*. London and New York: Methuen.

Light, P. (1986) 'The Social Concomitants of Role-Taking', in M. V. Cox *The Development of Cognition and Language*. Brighton: Harvester Press.

Little, V. (1989) 'Imagination and History' in J. Campbell and V. Little (eds.) *Humanities in the Primary School*. Lewes: Falmer Press.

Marbeau, L. (1988) 'History and Geography in School', in *Primary Education* 88, Vol. XX. No. 2.

Merriman, N. (1990) Curator, Museum of London in *The Times*, 23 August 1990.

Mink, L. O. (1968) 'Collingwood's Dialectic of History', in *History and Theory*. Vol. VII, No. 1.

Mitchell, R. and Middleton. G. (1967) *Living History Book One*. Holmes McDougall.

National Curriculum for History, Final Report (1990).

Noble, P. (1986) *The 17th Century*. Sussex: Ward Lock Educational.

Oliver, D. (1985) 'Language and Learning History', in *Education* 3–13. Vol. 13, No. 1.

Palmer, M. and Batho, G. (1981) 'The Source Method in History Teaching', *Teaching History Series*. The Historical Association, No. 48.

Parnes, S. H, (1959) 'Instructors Manual for Semester Courses in Creative Problem-Solving', Creative Education Foundation. Buffalo, New York.

Peel, E. A. (1960) *The Pupil's Thinking*. Oldbourne T.

Peel, E. A. (1967) in M. H. Burston and D. Thompson (eds.) *Studies in the Nature and Teaching of History*. London: Routledge.
Phenix, P. (1964) *Realms of Meaning*. London and New York: McGraw Hill.
Piaget, J. (1926) (3rd Edn 1959) *The Language and Thought of the Child*. London: Routledge.
Piaget, J. (1928) *Judgement and Reasoning in the Child*. London: Kegan Paul.
Piaget, J. (1932) *Moral Judgement and the Child*. London: Kegan Paul.
Piaget, J. (1950) *The Psychology of Intelligence*. London: Routledge and Kegan Paul.
Piaget, J. and Inhelder, B. (1951) *The Origin of the Idea of Chance in the Child*. London: Routledge.
Piaget, J. (1956) *A Child's Conception of Time*. London: Routledge.
Pocock, T. (1974) *Nelson and His World*. London: Thames and Hudson.
Pocock, T. (1987) *Horatio Nelson*. London: Bodley Head.
Plowden Report (1967) Children and their Primary Schools. Report of the Central Advisory Council for Education (England). London: HMSO.
Pring, R. (1976) *Knowledge and Schooling*. Wells: Open Books.
Prisk, T. (1987) 'Letting Them Get On With It: A Study of an Unsupervised Group Task in an Infant School', in A. Pollard *Children and their Primary Schools*. Lewis: Falmer Press.
Rees, A. (1976) 'Teaching Strategies for the Advancement and Development of Thinking Skills in History'. Unpub. MPhil Thesis. University of London.
Richmond, I. A. (1955) *Roman Britain*. Harmondsworth: Penguin.
Richmond, J. (1982) *The Resources of Classroom Language*. London: Arnold.
Rodney, W. (1972) *How Europe Underdeveloped Africa*. London: L'Ouverture Bogle.
Rogers, R. C. (1959) 'Towards a Theory of Creativity' in H. H. Anderson (ed.) *Creativity and its Cultivation*. Harper.
Rosen, C. and Rosen, H. (1973) *The Language of Primary School Children*. Harmondsworth: Penguin.
Rowbotham, S. (1973) *Hidden from History*. London: Pluto.
Ruddock, J. (1979) *Learning to Teach Through Discussion*. C.A.R.E. University of East Anglia.
Russell, J. (1981) 'Why "Socio-Cognitive Conflict" May be Impossible: The Status of Egocentric Errors in the Dyadic Performance of a Spatial Task', in *Education Psychology* 1, pp.159–69.
Ryle, G. (1979) *On Thinking*. Oxford: Blackwell.
Schools Council (1976–1978) *History 13–16*. Edinburgh: Holmes McDougall.
Schools Council (1979) *Learning through Talking 11–16*. London: Evans/Methuen Educational.
Schools Council (1975–1980) *History, Geography and Social Studies (8–13): Place, Time and Society*. London: Collins ESL.
Schools Council (1983) *Akbar and Elizabeth*. Schools Council Publications.
Sellars, W. C. and Yeatman, R. J. (1973) 1066 and all That. Harmondsworth: Penguin.

176

Shawyer, G., Booth, M. and Brown, R. (1988) 'The Development of Children's Historical Thinking', in *Cambridge Journal of Education*, Vol. 18, No. 2.

Shemilt, D. (1980) *History 13–16 Evaluation Study*. Edinburgh: Holmes McDougall.

Shif, Zh. (1935) *The Development of Scientific and Everyday Concepts*. Moscow: Uchpedgiz.

Speed, P. and Speed, M. (1987) *The Elizabethan Age, Books 1–4*. Oxford: Oxford University Press.

Smith, L. N. and Tomlinson, P. (1977) 'The Development of Children's Construction of Historical Duration', in *Educational Research*. Vol. 19, No. 3, pp.163–70.

Stones, E. (1979) *Psychopedagogy*. (Ch.9). London and New York: Methuen.

Strong, R. (1987) *Glorianna, The Portraits of Queen Elizabeth*. London: Thames and Hudson.

Sylvester, D. (1989) 'Children as Historians', in J. Campbell and V. Little (eds.) *Humanities in the Primary School*. Lewes: Falmer Press.

Thomas, K. (1983) *Man and the Natural World*. London: Allen Lane.

The Times Atlas of Ancient Civilizations (1989) Times Books/The Times.

Torrance, E. P. (1962) *Guiding Creative Talent*. London and New York: Prentice Hall.

Torrance, E. P. (1965) *Rewarding Creative Behaviour*. London and New York: Prentice Hall.

Uttley, A. (1977) *A Traveller in Time*. Harmondsworth: Puffin.

Unstead, R. J. (1964) *From Cavemen to Vikings*. London: A. and C. Black Ltd.

Vishram, R. (1988) *Ayars Lascars and Princes*. London: Pluto.

Vygotsky, L. S. (1962) *Thought and Language*. Edited and translated by E. Hanfmann and G. Vakar. London and New York: Wiley.

Wade, B. (1981) 'Assessing Pupils' Contributions in Appreciating a Poem', in *Journal of Education for Teaching* Vol. 7, No. 1, pp.40–9.

Wallach, M. A. and Kagan, N. (1965) *Modes of Thinking in Young Children*. London: Holt, Rinehart and Winston.

Watts, D. G. (1972) *The Learning of History*. London: Routledge and Kegan Paul.

Wedgwood, C. V. (1955) *The King's Peace 1637–1641 (The Great Rebellion)*. London: Collins.

Wedgwood, C. V. (1958) *The King's War 1641–1647*. London: Collins.

Werner, H. and Kaplan, E. (1963) *Symbol Formation, an Orgasmic Developmental Approach to Language and Expression of Thought*. London and New York: Wiley.

West, J. (1981) 'Children's Awareness of the Past', Unpub PhD Thesis. University of Keel.

Wood, D. and Middleton, D. (1975) 'A Study of Assisted Problem-Solving', in *British Journal of Psychology*. Vol. 66, pp.181–91.

Wright, D. (1984) 'A Small Local Investigation', in *Teaching History* No. 39. The Historical Association.

Index